EVIDENCES
OF THE
TRUE CHURCH

EVIDENCES

OF THE

TRUE CHURCH

DENNIS K. BROWN

This book is not an official publication of The Church of Jesus Christ of Latter-day Saints. The opinions and views expressed herein belong solely to the author and do not necessarily represent the opinions or views of Cedar Fort, Inc. Permission for the use of sources, graphics, and photos is also solely the responsibility of the author.

ISBN 13: 978-0-88290-712-3

Published by Horizon Publishers, an imprint of
Cedar Fort, Inc., 2373 W. 700 S., Springville, UT, 84663
Distributed by Cedar Fort, Inc., www.cedarfort.com

Cover design by Angela Olsen
Cover design © 2008 by Lyle Mortimer

Printed in the United States of America

10 9 8 7 6 5 4 3 2 1

Printed on acid-free paper

Contents

Foreword

During the 1990s I lived in Branson, Missouri and performed with my family, the Osmonds. While living there I formed the acquaintance of four direct descendants of the Prophet Joseph Smith who were members of the Hedrickite Church, an early break-off of The Church of Jesus Christ of Latter-day Saints. The Hedrickites currently own a portion of the Temple Lot in Independence, Missouri, where, we believe, a great temple will be built prior to the Second Coming of the Savior Jesus Christ.

I had a number of discussions with these acquaintances about the teachings of the Church and my testimony of their truthfulness, but they showed little interest. Around this same time a friend sent me a copy of a talk on the Dead Sea Scrolls given by Dennis Brown, whom I didn't know. I was fascinated by the conclusions I read and I located Dennis to confirm the references for the statements in his talk about the amazing and incredible evidences of the Church found in the Scrolls.

I gave copies of the talk to my acquaintances. They immediately showed an interest in wanting to know more about Heavenly Father's revelations to their ancestor, Joseph Smith, and in the teachings of The Church of Jesus Christ of Latter-day Saints. They were taught the doctrines of the Church, they prayed, and received a testimony of their truthfulness. In late 1999 I baptized these four friends into the Church.

The talk on the Dead Sea Scrolls is summarized in Chapter Three of this book. Throughout my life I have been interested in the many evidences of the true church. They strengthen my faith and they help interest our friends and neighbors in the Church and the Gospel of Jesus Christ and the Plan of our Heavenly Father.

My testimony, however, is not based on these evidences. I have felt the witness of the Holy Ghost, which has spoken to my heart and mind on many occasions, about the truthfulness of the Church. It has spoken to me as a soft, still voice as well as by a strong burning feeling, like being wrapped in a warm, peaceful blanket. It has strengthened me and lifted me and taught me and protected me.

I have performed with the Osmond Family and the Osmond Brothers for over 40 years. We have performed around the world, on many thousands of occasions, for crowds of tens of thousands, as well as in private audiences for kings, queens, presidents, and leaders of nations. We have been surrounded by those who are famous, those who are rich, and those who are powerful. In all of these surroundings, however, I have found that there is nothing so wonderful as the sweet, peaceful assurance of the closeness of my Heavenly Father, of the reality of the Atonement of the Savior Jesus Christ, and of the witness of the Holy Ghost that the teachings of the Church are true.

I invite all to come unto Christ, to follow his teachings, and to seek the witness of the Spirit of the truthfulness of the things taught in this book.

—Merrill Osmond

Preface

The Spirit of the Holy Ghost has borne witness to me numerous times that Joseph Smith was a prophet of God, that *The Book of Mormon* is the divine word of God, and that The Church of Jesus Christ of Latter-day Saints is led by our Savior Jesus Christ. The greatest proof of all is the feeling inside us, which is the witness of the Spirit. President Gordon B. Hinckley has said that the proof of *The Book of Mormon* is found within its pages.

Bruce R. McConkie said:

We do not come to a knowledge of God and his laws through intellectuality, or by research, or by reason. Joseph Smith said that a man could learn more about the things of God by looking into heaven for five minutes than by reading all the books ever written upon the subject of religion.[1]

I have found that my testimony and the testimonies of others have been greatly strengthened by studying and analyzing the many evidences of the truthfulness of the Church. As one writer penned: "What no one shows the ability to defend is quickly abandoned. Rational argument does not create belief, but it maintains a climate in which belief may flourish."[2]

John W. Welch, founder of the Foundation of Ancient Research and Mormon Studies (FARMS), said: "Without diminishing the essential power of the Holy Ghost in bearing testimony, and knowing that we cannot prove anything in absolute terms, I still speak favorably about the power of evidence. It is an important ingredient in Heavenly Father's plan of happiness."[3] Elder Boyd K. Packer said: "Each of us must accommodate the mixture of reason and revelation in our lives. The gospel not only permits but requires it."[4]

Over the past several years many books and articles have been written on selected evidences of the truthfulness of the Gospel. Most of these books have focused on *The Book of Mormon* with a few on other subjects such as the Dead Sea Scrolls and ancient temples. These are three of the eleven subjects that will be treated in this book.

Most of the evidence or proof documented herein has come to light in just the past two decades. In 1976 Elder Neal A. Maxwell predicted: "There will be a convergence of discoveries (never enough, mind you, to remove the need for faith) to make plain and plausible what the modern prophets have been saying all along."[5] This has surely come to pass. This book was written to summarize much of the evidence already documented and to add my analysis and reasoning to many more items of proof. As can be seen in these pages, there are literally hundreds of items that verify the truthfulness of the Church and the Gospel.

I first became interested in the evidence of truthfulness of the Gospel and the Church during my mission to France and Belgium in the 1960s when I read some of Dr. Hugh Nibley's excellent works and Jack H. West's articles called, "The Trial of the Stick of Joseph" which were published in the *Improvement Era*. My interest has flourished over the years and I have since read many hundreds of books and articles on the various items of proof of the Gospel.

A few days after the First Vision in 1820, Joseph Smith told a protestant minister about the marvelous manifestation that he had experienced. Of that experience the Prophet later wrote: "I was greatly surprised at his behavior; he treated my communication not only lightly, but with great contempt, saying it was all of the devil."[6] From that time forward the Church has been strongly criticized in every way imaginable. Even aspects of the Church which to me are clear evidences of the truth are criticized. The prophets have often reminded us that the strength of the Church is in the testimonies of its members.

My research and the writing of this book have brought my soul closer to my Savior Jesus Christ. It has been well worth the more than thirty years of effort I have put into this work. If it motivates even one single person to search out the witness of the Spirit, I will be doubly blessed.

Notes

1. McConkie, Bruce R., "The Lord's People Receive Revelation," April 1971 General Conference, *Ensign,* The Church of Jesus Christ of Latter-day Saints, Salt Lake City, May 1971.
2. Farrar, Austin, "The Christian Apologist," *Light on C. S. Lewis,* Gibb, Jocelyn Ed., New York, Harcourt, Brace and World, 1965, p. 26.
3. Welch, John W., *The Power of Evidence in the Nurturing of Faith,* FARMS, Provo, Utah, 1995; p. 149.
4. Packer, Boyd K., "'I Say unto You, Be One' (Doctrine and Covenants, 38:27)," *Devotionals and Fireside Speeches,* Brigham Young University, Provo, Utah, 1991, p. 89.
5. Maxwell, Neal A., *Deposition of a Disciple,* Deseret Book, Salt Lake City, 1976, p. 49.
6. Smith, Joseph, *Joseph Smith History* 1:21, The Pearl of Great Price, The Church of Jesus Christ of Latter-day Saints, Salt Lake City, 1981.

1
Jesus Christ

As members of The Church of Jesus Christ of Latter-day Saints, we worship our Heavenly Father in the name of Jesus Christ, who is our Savior and Redeemer. We know that it is only through the atoning blood of Christ that we may return to our Father in Heaven.

There are more than 20,800 Christian churches in the world today. Many leaders and members of these churches assert that Mormons are not Christian. We say, "*of course,* we are." We believe that Jesus Christ is the Son of God. We accept him as our Savior and Redeemer. In fact, the proper name of our church is The Church of Jesus Christ of Latter-day Saints.

Others then say, "Well, you do not believe in the same Christ in whom we believe."

In many ways, that is true. We do not. So, it can rightly be said that according to the other Christians in the world and their definition of what Jesus Christ is and was, we are not Christian.

In the first part of this chapter I discuss several important points that demonstrate that our beliefs about Jesus Christ are different from those of the Christian world, but they do indeed provide evidence of the true Church. In the second part of this chapter I describe our specific beliefs about the Savior's Atonement and how those beliefs differ from the teachings of other Christian churches. I also discuss the great importance of the Atonement in the lives of each of us.

Let me first describe seven aspects of the Christ whom we revere, which are different from the Christ of the Christian world:

First, we believe that Jesus Christ, our Savior, has a glorified, resurrected body of flesh and bones today. A few years ago, I became a close friend with a protestant minister in Denver, Colorado. At times I took my family to his church and he brought his family to ours. Frequently we discussed religion and I presented him with a copy of *The Book of Mormon* and LeGrand Richards' *A Marvelous Work and a Wonder.* I requested that he listen to our missionaries.

One day I told my friend about the appearance of God the Father and Jesus Christ to Joseph Smith, who saw them as Glorified Personages. The protestant minister said, "My concept of God and Jesus Christ is different from yours. Don't you believe in a God as a spirit without a body who is emotionless, who can be found everywhere but is not really anywhere, who fills the whole universe but is small enough to fill an individual's heart?"

I responded to his question by saying, "I cannot even understand that description."

My friend said, "Well, that is what is so beautiful about God."

We believe what is taught in the Old Testament, that we are created in the image of God (Genesis 1:27). If God is an incomprehensible spirit, then how could it be that we are created in his image?

Following his resurrection, the Savior appeared to the apostles he'd chosen with a glorified body. He said, "Behold my hands and my feet, that it is I myself: handle me, and see; for a spirit hath not flesh and bones, as ye see me have" (Luke 24:39). We also know that Jesus will return to the earth in the same form as he ascended into heaven (Acts 1:11). He still has his resurrected body. To deny that Christ has a resurrected body of flesh and bones is to deny the resurrection itself, which overcame physical death. Then it would logically follow that neither was the atonement of Jesus Christ real.

Second, we believe that Jesus Christ is a separate being from God the Father, and also from the Holy Ghost. Many Christians accept the Nicene Creed, which came into being by a vote of priests in the fourth century A.D. The Athanasian creed, a subsequent version of the Nicene Creed, states that:

> The Godhead of the Father, Son and Holy Ghost is all one. . . . The Father [is] incomprehensible, the Son incomprehensible, and the Holy Ghost incomprehensible. The Father [is] eternal, the Son eternal, [and] the Holy Ghost eternal. And yet there are not three eternals; but one eternal. As also there are not three incomprehensibles . . . but one incomprehensible. The Father is God, the Son is God, and the Holy Ghost is God, and yet they are not three Gods but one God.

When Jesus was baptized in the River Jordan, a voice came from heaven that said, "This is my beloved Son, in whom I am well pleased" (Matthew 3:17). The Holy Ghost appeared in the form of a dove. It was obvious that Jesus was separate from the Father and from the Holy Ghost.

Throughout his life, Jesus prayed to his father. He did not, of course, pray to himself. In the Garden of Gethsemane, he said, "Not my will, but thine be done." How could the Father, Son and Holy Ghost be one? It can only be that they are one in purpose.

After Christ ascended into heaven, Stephen was stoned for his beliefs in his Redeemer. During that event, he looked up and beheld the Savior standing at the right hand of the Father (Acts 7:55). When the Father and Son appeared to Joseph Smith, Jesus was also standing at the side of God the Father.

Third, we believe that Jesus Christ is the head of the Church he organized. It included apostles and prophets, which the Bible says the Church must have until everyone comes to a unity of the faith (Ephesians 4:11-13). His Church also included the Melchizedek Priesthood and the Aaronic Priesthood (Hebrews 7:11) and a number of priesthood offices such as high priests (Hebrews 5:10) and seventies (Luke 10:1).

We believe the Savior's true Church is organized the same way today as he organized it when he was here on earth. However, there is no other church besides ours that is organized in the same manner as his. Protestants generally believe that if an individual accepts Jesus and "confesses" that he is the Christ, the specific church is not important. But how can there be more than one true church? If two churches teach conflicting doctrines, certainly they cannot both be right. Paul said, "One Lord, one faith, one baptism" (Ephesians 4:5). When the early apostles met believers who had been baptized by someone without authority, they rebaptized them (Acts 19).

Fourth, we believe that Jesus Christ gave his apostles priesthood authority to act in his name. That authority remained with the Lord's chosen church leaders when he was crucified and resurrected, leaving the earth with such authority to function. When the Savior chose his twelve apostles, he laid his hands on their heads and said, "You have not chosen me, but I have chosen you and ordained you" (John 15:16). They subsequently ordained bishops, elders and other officers in the Church.

The Catholic Church claims to have a direct line of ordained popes back to Peter. However, they readily admit that in the several different lines they claim, there have been periods where there was no pope. Also, there have been some wicked popes and during some periods there were even two or three popes at the same time.

The Apostle John wrote the Gospel of John, the three Epistles of John and the Book of Revelation thirty to forty years after Peter died. John never mentioned another head of the Church, who was supposedly the bishop of Rome. Neither did any other historian or religious writer in the second and third centuries A.D. refer to such a church leader. These revelations were not given to the bishop of Rome.

The Protestants do not believe Catholics have a valid priesthood line. Since all Protestants broke off from the Catholic Church, they don't believe any priesthood line is necessary.

Every male member of our Church who holds the priesthood has a direct line back to Jesus Christ, the head of this Church. We hold the direct authority to act in the name of Christ.

Fifth, we believe that Jesus Christ sent the Holy Ghost to guide us in his absence. Jesus said that in order to enter the Kingdom of God everyone must be born of water and of the spirit (John 3:5). Being born of the water means to be baptized by immersion by one holding the priesthood authority. Being born of the Spirit is to receive the Holy Ghost through the priesthood by the laying on of hands (Acts 8:17).

The Holy Ghost is our Comforter, Protector, and Teacher who testifies of Jesus Christ. We receive him as a gift, which is different than the Light of Christ, which is given to all of God's children as they are born into the world (John 1: 9) and is the source of spiritual feelings experienced by many good and honorable people who are living today.

I have often asked people of other faiths if they could testify that they have a spiritual assurance that their church is true, the only true church as it was organized by Jesus Christ. I have yet to meet a single one who would so testify. Members of The Church of Jesus Christ of Latter-day Saints testify that they have received the Holy Ghost and the witness that the Church is directed by Jesus Christ himself.

Sixth, we believe that Jesus Christ gave us a second witness of his divinity. In the Bible it says: "In the mouth of two or three witnesses shall every word be established" (2 Corinthians 13:1). Matthew 18:16 also states: "In the mouth of two or three witnesses every word may be established." This is again stated in First Timothy 5:19. It is also stated in the Old Testament in Deuteronomy 17:6 and 19:15.

Today we have the writings of the prophets of the New Testament as a witness of the divinity of the Savior Jesus Christ. As a second witness, we have the writings of the prophets of The Book of Mormon. Jesus said he was going to visit "other sheep not of this fold" (John 10:16). Other churches do not understand what the Savior was talking about here. In The Book of Mormon Jesus explained that the people who lived on the American continents were the "other sheep" (3 Nephi 15:21).

Ezekiel 37:16-19 says there will be two records: The record of Judah and the record of Joseph, which would become one. All Christian churches teach that the Bible is the record of Judah, but no other church knows where to find the record of Joseph. We are greatly blessed to have The Book of Mormon, which is the record of Joseph and a second witness of Jesus Christ.

Seventh, we believe that Jesus Christ is alive today and is actively directing his Church here on earth. Many ask why we do not have crosses in our homes and on our churches like other Christian churches. We generally do not think of Jesus Christ dying on the cross. We think of him alive in the garden after his resurrection. We think of him in Gethsemane where he bled from every pore as a result of our sins that he had taken upon him. We revere Jesus Christ as our Savior who is alive today, and who is directing us through his ordained apostles and prophets.

Jesus appeared to Joseph Smith in 1820; he spoke to Oliver Cowdery, David Whitmer and Martin Harris in 1829 (The Testimony of the Three Witnesses); he appeared to Joseph and Sidney Rigdon in 1832 (D&C 76); he appeared to Joseph and Oliver Cowdery in the Kirtland Temple in 1836 (D&C 110); and he appeared to Joseph along with several others during this period.

The first time I entered the Salt Lake Temple, I was in the hallway outside of the Celestial Room when a temple worker came up and said that where I stood was the very place the Savior appeared to Lorenzo Snow in 1898. During a particularly spiritual meeting, if someone said to President Harold B. Lee that the veil was especially thin that day, President Lee would respond, "What veil?" or "There is no veil."[1]

If we must accept the rest of the Christian world's definition of Jesus Christ, we are not Christian. We believe in the Christ of the Holy Scriptures and we revere him as our Redeemer. As Nephi said in the Book of Mormon, "And we talk of Christ, we rejoice in

Christ, we preach of Christ, we prophesy of Christ . . . that our children may know to what source they may look for a remission of their sins" (2 Nephi 25:26). We are the Lord's disciples. We strive to live like him. We strive to love others as he did.

The second part of this chapter has to do with our beliefs regarding the Atonement of the Savior. These beliefs, too, are different from the beliefs of the Christian world. Because of the importance of this subject, I have separated it from some of the other differences in our beliefs.

In the Church, we preach the Gospel or the "good news." The Bible Dictionary defines "Gospel" in one sentence: "The *good news* is that Jesus Christ has made a perfect atonement for mankind that will redeem all mankind from the grave and reward each individual according to his/her works" (p. 682).

At Christmas, we celebrate the birth of Jesus in Bethlehem. At Easter, we rejoice in his life and resurrection. We cannot separate the purpose of his birth from the purpose of his life nor from the purpose of his death. They are all tied together in the plan of our Heavenly Father. This link is the Atonement or the *at-one-ment*, which is the key to our *becoming one with* and returning to our Heavenly Father. The Atonement is tied to the Creation, the Fall, to Gethsemane, the cross and to the Resurrection.

At the culmination of the Creation, Adam and Eve were placed in the Garden of Eden. Their bodies had no blood. They could not grow old or die. They were in a paradisiacal state and were unable to multiply and replenish the earth as God commanded them in order for us to come here (2 Nephi 2:23, Alma 12:21-23). It was necessary for every one of Heavenly Father's children to come to the earth in order to gain a body, to form a family unit, to gain experiences and to be tested so we could return to our Heavenly Father and become like him.

The only way Adam and Eve could multiply and be tested was to obtain a mortal body and be removed from the presence of God. The only way to get out of his presence was to break or transgress a commandment. (A transgression is breaking one commandment by obeying a higher one.) Without such a transgression they would remain in his presence. Under the law of the agency of man, Heavenly Father would never force any of his children to do anything.

The commandment to multiply and replenish the earth was in conflict with God's instruction to not partake of the fruit of the tree of knowledge of good and evil. In light of the statement by Nephi (1 Nephi 3:7) that the Lord would not require his children to do anything without providing a way for them to do what he has commanded, the instruction to not partake of the fruit of the tree of knowledge of good and evil must not have been a commandment in the same degree as the commandment to multiply and replenish the earth. Adam and Eve chose to obey the greater of the two, which was to multiply and replenish the earth. This resulted in what became known as the Fall.

The Fall

As a result of Adam and Eve's transgression, blood started flowing in their bodies and they became susceptible to disease, to aging and to death. Adam and Eve were told that in the day they were to eat of the fruit, they would surely die. He meant, of course, that they would become mortal and that in a true sense, they began to die from the time they partook of the fruit.

Also, since they had transgressed, they had to be removed from the presence of God since no unclean thing can be in his kingdom (3 Nephi 27:19). To be removed from the presence of God is to suffer a *spiritual death*. The Fall caused that all the children of Adam and Eve (which is all who have ever lived or will live here on earth) should suffer spiritual death. Since all of us are deprived of being in the presence of our Heavenly Father we will each, through our agency, inevitably make mistakes and sin. Therefore, Adam and Eve and all their descendants will sin and die, suffering both spiritual and physical death.

Living in this mortal world will bring physical death and the only way physical death could be overcome is for one of God's children to provide a resurrection. The only person who could do this was the One who was not required to do so, God's Only Begotten Son, Jesus Christ. He had the power to choose to live or die, thereby exercising the law of agency.

Justice requires payment for sin. If we had to pay for our own sins, it would be like a debtors' prison or hell from which we could never escape. Being out of the presence of God, we would continue to sin. The only other person who could pay for our sins was the One who was perfect, who was without sin. He could choose to pay for our sins, thereby exercising the law of agency. By doing so, his mercy toward us satisfies the law of justice.

The Life of Christ

Jesus, who was born in Bethlehem, was the literal son of God the Father and Mary. He possessed both the heavenly attributes of God and the earthly attributes of man. He volunteered in the pre-earth life to pay for the transgression of Adam, which had resulted in physical death for all of God's children, and which was conquered by Christ's resurrection. He voluntarily allowed himself to be crucified, then resurrected on the third day, having overcome physical death.

He paid for our sins by first living a perfect life, then voluntarily shedding his blood in the Garden of Gethsemane. Our sins came about because of our agency that allowed us to choose good or evil. Mortality came as the result of Adam's transgression. Using his agency, Jesus Christ paid for the sins of man and overcame mortality, or physical death.

The Atonement, the Crucifixion, and the Resurrection

The word "Gethsemane" means "oil and/or wine press." Today in Jerusalem one can see many large stones that were used to crush olives to form pure or virgin olive oil or grapes to produce juice and/or wine. The Savior, who was born of a virgin, went to Gethsemane to be crushed by the weight of our sins. He did not have to suffer for any personal sins since he was perfect, however, he chose to suffer for our sins. Today we use pure olive oil in anointing the sick as a symbol of the Atonement in Gethsemane. We use wine (or, in these latter days, water) in the sacrament as a symbol of his atoning sacrifice.

The Scriptures say that in the Garden, Christ fell on his face, so great was the weight of our sins. He cried out, "Abba," which is a term of endearment, like "Daddy." On the cross, when he said, "My God, my God, why hast thou forsaken me?" (Matthew 27:46), the Spirit of God left him that, alone, he might know what it is to live without it and that he might make the required payment for sin totally on his own. In the Garden he bled from every pore and, by so doing, he paid for our sins. The Book of Mormon teaches us that he not only took upon him our sins, but also our illnesses, our afflictions, our worries, our problems, and our suffering (Alma 7:11-12).

When Jesus was taken away before his crucifixion, he was scourged with a whip with talons hooked to sharp objects, which were meant to tear the skin and cause great bleeding. It was standard to whip a prisoner thirty-nine times. By itself, this could drain sufficient blood to die, making subsequent death through crucifixion come more quickly. The Romans did not know, however, that in the Garden Jesus had already bled from every pore.

When Adam and Eve left the Garden of Eden and suffered spiritual death, blood began flowing in their bodies. In paying for spiritual death, Jesus paid with his blood. He bled from every pore; he bled further by the scourging and by the crown of thorns. On the cross, a sword pierced his side causing blood and water to come out (John 19:34).

On the third day, as prophesied, Jesus rose from the grave, having overcome death and providing all men in immortality the blessing of resurrection. The resurrection was for all mankind, for an infinite number of worlds. Jesus's Atonement was an infinite one— infinite in suffering and infinite in scope. That is why it is truly said that he suffered for the sins of all mankind.

The word "atonement" in Hebrew means "to cover" or "to forgive." In Aramaic and Arabic, it means "a close embrace."[2] Lehi said, "the Lord hath redeemed my soul . . . I have beheld his glory, and I am encircled about eternally in the arms of his love" (2 Nephi 1:15). Mormon, Alma and Amulek spoke of being "clasped in the arms of Jesus" (Mormon 5:11; Alma 5:33; 34:16). I look forward to that day, to be clasped in his arms and to be one with him.

Ordinances

The ordinances of the Gospel symbolize the Atonement of Jesus Christ and are the keys to effecting the Atonement in our lives. The first key, *baptism*, symbolizes the Atonement, specifically the death and resurrection of Jesus Christ. The Bible says:

> Know ye not, that so many of us as were baptized into Jesus Christ were baptized into his death? Therefore we are buried with him by baptism into death; that like as Christ was raised up from the dead by the glory of the Father, even so we also should walk in newness of life. For if we have been planted together in the likeness of his death, we shall be also in the likeness of his resurrection (Romans 6:3-5).

Just as the Savior died and was placed in the tomb, so we are immersed in the waters of baptism. As he rose anew from the grave, so we rise from the waters anew, cleansed from our sins and ready to begin a new life of righteous living. Clearly, baptism is essential to enter into the kingdom of heaven (See John 3:5 and Mark 16:16).

When other churches fail to baptize, or do so by sprinkling, or when they baptize without the proper authority, they miss this essential ingredient of the Atonement. No matter how good the life is that people may live, they still need the ordinance of baptism in order to return to their Heavenly Father.

The second key, the **sacrament**, also symbolizes the Atonement. The bread we eat is in remembrance of the body of Christ, which was resurrected. The resurrection brought to pass the immortality of all mankind. It was solely by his grace and mercy that we will live again. When I partake of the bread I think of how he was crucified and resurrected for all mankind, thereby paying for the sin of Adam.

The water we drink is in remembrance of the blood of Christ which was shed as part of the Atonement in the Garden of Gethsemane. This is how he brought to pass eternal life for you and me, which results from our repentance and his mercy, along with our good works. When I drink of the water, I think of the Garden and how he paid for my sins.

"This is my work and my glory—to bring to pass the immortality and eternal life of man" (Moses 1:39). *Immortality* is brought about by the *resurrection*, which is for everyone and can be symbolized with the bread. *Eternal life* can result from the *Atonement*, which is for you and me and everyone else who will repent, which is symbolized by the wine or the water.

Bread	*Wine or Water*
body	blood
resurrection	atonement
immortality	eternal life

The third key that is symbolized by the Atonement is the ordinances in the **temple**. The entire endowment ceremony in the temple symbolizes the Atonement of Jesus Christ beginning with the Creation, the Fall and the Redemption. Through these we are able to return to our Heavenly Father. Through the Atonement, mercy satisfies justice. The Creation required the Fall. The Fall required the Atonement. The Atonement fulfilled the purposes of the Creation. Once we understand the Atonement, even in a small way, we will always be grateful to our Savior.

The Atonement has two parts. First, it overcomes the transgression of Adam, which brought the death of the physical body. The Savior's resurrection provided that everyone who has ever lived will be resurrected. "For as in Adam all die even so in Christ shall all be made alive" (1 Corinthians 15:22).

The second part of the Atonement provides that if we will repent and strive to keep the commandments, the Savior paid for our sins so we can literally return to our Heavenly Father. By the grace and mercy of Jesus Christ we are saved, but it requires good works on our part to bring about our salvation or exaltation. Without the Atonement there is no way we could ever overcome the effect of our sins. Being sinful, there is no way we could ever return to our Heavenly Father without the atoning sacrifice of our Savior. Jesus is our Savior, our Redeemer and the Messiah.

Stephen Robinson, a professor of religion at Brigham Young University told the following story about his daughter. He was sitting in a chair in his living room reading the newspaper when Sarah, his seven-year-old daughter, asked, "Daddy, can I get a bike? I'm the only kid in our neighborhood who doesn't have a bike."

Brother Robinson answered, "You save all your pennies, and pretty soon you'll have enough for a bike."

Some time later he heard a "clink, clink" in Sarah's bedroom. He went to her room and asked what she was doing. She said, "You promised that if I saved all my pennies, pretty soon I'd have enough to get a bike. And Daddy, I've saved every single one."

"Okay, Sarah," Brother Robinson said, "let's go downtown and look at bikes."

The two of them went to every store in town and she finally found the perfect bicycle. She said, "Dad, this is it. This is just the one I want." Then she looked at the price tag. It cost more than $100. The little girl began to cry. "Oh Daddy, I'll never have enough for a bicycle!"

Brother Robinson was touched by his daughter's sadness and said, "Sarah, how much money do you have?"

She answered, "Sixty-one cents." He said, "Well, I'll tell you what. You give me everything you've got, the whole sixty-one cents, and a hug and a kiss, and this bike is yours."[3]

This is somewhat like the Atonement. Since we are all mortal and we sin on a continual basis, and since we all require constant repentance, we will always come up short, no matter how much we have and no matter how much good we have done. But if we give everything we have—all our good works—the Savior will take care of the rest (2 Nephi 25:23).

As members of The Church of Jesus Christ of Latter-day Saints, we are Christians, whatever the rest of the world might say. As Nephi said: "We talk of Christ, we rejoice in Christ, we preach of Christ, we prophesy of Christ" (2 Nephi 25:26).

Notes:

1. Walsh, Jack, "D. Arthur Haycock: Aide to Four Prophets," *Ensign*, The Church of Jesus Christ of Latter-day Saints, Salt Lake City, August 1984; p. 24.
2. Nelson, Russell M., October 1996 General Conference, "The Atonement," *Ensign*, The Church of Jesus Christ of Latter-day Saints, Salt Lake City, November 1996; p. 34.
3. Robinson, Stephen, *Believing Christ*, Deseret Book, Salt Lake City, 1992; pp. 30-32.

2
The Bible

*The Holy Bible provides a blueprint for finding the true Church
of Jesus Christ.*

Some time ago, a protestant minister in Denver, Colorado wrote
a letter to the editor of the Rocky Mountain News, stating that the
Mormon Church could not be true because it teaches doctrines that
are not in the Bible, such as baptism for the dead and the wearing of
secret temple garments. I would like to respond to this minister.

First let me talk about baptism for the dead. Christ, while on the
cross, said to one of the thieves at his side, "Today shalt thou be with
me in paradise" (Luke 23:43). After his ordeal, on the third day,
Christ said to Mary Magdalene: "Touch me not; for I am not yet
ascended to my Father" (John 20:17). Therefore, paradise is not the
place where our Heavenly Father dwells.

What did Christ do during those two days after his crucifixion?
The answer is that "He went and preached unto the spirits in
prison"(1 Peter 3:19, 20). These were those who had lived at the
time of Noah. "For this cause was the gospel preached also to them
that are dead, that they might be judged according to men in the
flesh" (1 Peter 4:6). Christ was teaching the Gospel to the people
who drowned at the time of Noah, that they might have the same
chance as those who receive the Gospel in the flesh.

Baptism is essential for salvation (Mark 16:16). "Except a man
be born of water and of the Spirit, he cannot enter into the kingdom
of God" (John 3:5). Therefore, the spirits whom Christ was teaching in paradise or spirit prison also required baptism in order to enter
into the kingdom of God. This was true even if they accepted the
Gospel. So, how can a spirit be baptized when baptism is an earthly ordinance requiring that the body be immersed in water? How
could a spirit be baptized?

The answer is that those who remain alive on the earth are baptized by proxy for those who are dead and have passed on to paradise, as the Savior called it when he was hanging on the cross and

spoke to the thief at his side. If those who have died accept the Gospel after death, they will have a valid baptism performed by us in mortality on their behalf. This is a beautiful doctrine that demonstrates God's mercy and compassion toward his children. Everyone who has ever lived on this earth will have an opportunity to accept or reject the Gospel of Jesus Christ and to receive the blessings of baptism, even if this ordinance requires those who remain alive on earth to do it by proxy.

This doctrine is mentioned in the Bible. Speaking of the resurrection, Paul said, "Else what shall they do which are baptized for the dead, if the dead rise not at all? Why are they then baptized for the dead?" (1 Corinthians 15:29). Although this doctrine is in the Bible, to my knowledge, no other church on earth practices it.

I have an old French Bible that was translated in the early 1600s. The Catholic Church makes the claim that this translation of the Bible is more accurate than the King James Version. In this Bible the footnote to the scripture quoted from Corinthians says, "We do not know what the doctrine of baptism for the dead was."

(Incidentally, another footnote in this Bible is interesting. Revelations 14:6, 7 says: "And I saw another angel fly in the midst of heaven, having the everlasting gospel to preach unto them that dwell on the earth." Referring to this scripture, the Church teaches that Moroni was that angel carrying The Book of Mormon. The footnote to this verse in this old Catholic Bible states that the "everlasting gospel" brought by the angel is a book that is to come forth.)

Second, as to temple clothes, the Bible tells us: Adam and Eve sewed fig leaves together and made themselves aprons (Genesis 3:7). "Unto Adam also and to his wife did the Lord God make coats of skins, and clothed them." (Genesis 3:21). The Bible speaks of "The cloths of service, to do service in the holy place, the holy garments for Aaron the priest, and the garments of his sons, to minister in the priest's office" (Exodus 35:19). "And they came, every one whose heart stirred him up . . . and they brought the Lord's offering to the work of the tabernacle . . . and for the holy garments." (Exodus 35:21). "And he put upon him the coat, and girded him with the girdle and clothed him with the robe" (Leviticus 8:7).

There are many other doctrines mentioned in the Bible, which, to my knowledge, we alone teach. There may be an isolated church of which I am not aware that preaches one or more of the following, but to my knowledge, not one of the 20,800 other Christian churches in the world today preaches even a single one of the following doctrines.

We should have apostles and prophets until we come in the unity of the faith (Ephesians 2:20 and 4:11-13). I find it strange that no other church has apostles. You would think they would be organized like the church Christ organized. God always communicates through prophets (Amos 3:7). No other church believes in modern-day prophets.

The true Church should have the Melchizedek Priesthood (Hebrews 6:20). No other church has a Melchizedek Priesthood. Likewise, it should have the Levitical Priesthood after the order of Aaron (Hebrews 7:11). It should have high priests (Hebrews 5:10), and seventies (Luke 10:1). No other church has high priests or seventies. The true Church should have temples (Malachi 3:1). No other church has temples as described in the Bible. The Church should teach about three kingdoms of glory, including the Celestial and Terrestrial kingdoms (1 Corinthians 15:40,41); 2 Corinthians 12:2 also talks about being caught up into the third heaven. No other church teaches about three kingdoms of glory in the hereafter. Jeremiah 1:5 talks about the pre-earth life. No other church believes in this.

I quoted earlier from Luke and First Peter about paradise and spirit prison. No other church teaches about these. The laying on of hands for the gift of the Holy Ghost is mentioned (Acts 8:17). No other church has this doctrine for its members. We are literally the spirit children of God (Romans 8:16). We alone teach this. Christ has a resurrected body of flesh and bones (Luke 24:39) and Genesis 1:27 says we were created in God's image. No one else teaches that God has a body today.

Matthew 16:19 talks about sealing in heaven. No other church teaches about sealing or eternal marriage. The Bible says we can become gods (Romans 8:17 and Psalms 82:6). Other churches say this is blasphemy. Jesus said he had other sheep that were not part of the fold during his lifetime whom he would teach after his resurrection (John 10:16), and Ezekiel 37:16 speaks of the Stick of Joseph that would come forth. No other church has an explanation for these scriptures.

Hebrews 5:4 says that an officer in the Church must be called as was Aaron, that is, called by a prophet and ordained by the laying on of hands. No other church preaches that its officers must be called by modern-day prophets. Members of the church at the time of Christ were called saints (Romans 1:7; 1 Corinthians 1:2; Ephesians 1:1; 2 Corinthians 1:1; Philippians 1:1; and Colossians 1:2). No other church today refers to its members as saints.

Matthew 3:16, 17, Luke 22:42 and many other scriptures clearly say that Jesus Christ is a separate being from God the Father and from the Holy Ghost. We alone teach this. I think it is incredible that, to my knowledge, not a single other Christian church preaches even one of the above doctrines.

There are many additional doctrines in the Bible that are taught by a few other Christian churches but are not taught by the overwhelming majority. Some of these include James 5:14 that says that when members of the Church are ill, they should call for the elders who will anoint them with oil. Only a few other churches do this. Malachi 3:8 mentions tithing. Out of 20,800 other Christian churches, only a handful teach about tithing. The word "tithe" itself means to pay a tenth part of one's increase.

John 3:5 and Mark 16:16 teach clearly that everyone must be baptized to enter into the Kingdom of God. Only selected Christian churches preach this. Baptism must be performed by immersion (Matthew 3:16; Mark 1:10; John 3:23; and Acts 8:38). The word "baptism" comes from a Greek word meaning to immerse. Only a few churches teach this. We should partake of bread and drink in remembrance of the Savior (Matthew 26:26, 27; and 1 Corinthians 11:24-26). Only certain churches do this.

First Timothy 3:2 says that bishops must be married. This is frequently not the case in some other churches, which teach that bishops should be celibate and single.

It is interesting that the doctrines forming the base of most of the doctrines and beliefs of other Christian churches are not in the Bible. These include doctrines such as infant baptism, baptism by sprinkling, the doctrine of "original sin" where all must pay for the sin of Adam, a paid and unmarried clergy, and heaven and hell as the only possible rewards of living on the earth.

The minister to whom I referred at the beginning of this chapter, in the article that appeared in the newspaper, also said that The Church of Jesus Christ of Latter-day Saints preaches things that are not in the Bible. This is true, but there are at least two reasons for this. First, there are many apparent contradictions in the Bible. This is one of the reasons why there are more than 20,800 different

Christian churches today, each one teaching its own interpretation of the scriptures. There have been many mistranslations of the Bible over the centuries. Our church has a prophet to clarify these important doctrines and to teach us the truth about things that have been confusing due to the translations of men.

A second reason we teach things that are not in the Bible is that nowhere in the Holy Bible does it purport to be the complete word of God. The word "bible" comes from the Greek "biblios," which means "books" or "collection of books." The Bible was not totally compiled until the fourth century after Christ. At that time there existed numerous records written by many prophets. The selection of records to be included in the Bible was somewhat arbitrary and has been inconsistent among the many versions of the Bible that have been translated and published. The Catholic Bible today, for example, contains fifteen more books, and the Greek Orthodox Bible contains twenty-seven more books than the King James Version.

There are many writings that are not included in any of the current versions. The Bible itself mentions other books, which are not included, such as the Book of Enoch (Jude 1:14), the Book of Jasher (Joshua 10:13) the Book of the Acts of Solomon (1 Kings 11:41), the Book of The Covenant (Exodus 24:7), the Book of the Wars of the Lord (Numbers 21:14), the Book of Samuel the Seer (1 Chronicles 29:29), the Book of Nathan the Prophet (2 Chronicles 9:29), the Book of Shemaiah the Prophet (2 Chronicles 12:15), the third epistle to the Corinthians (1 Corinthians 5:9), and the epistle from Laodicea (Colossians 4:16).

Recent findings such as the Dead Sea Scrolls and the Nag Hammadi Codices contain several hundred important religious writings besides those that are in our current versions of the Bible and that the people in ancient times believed were as sacred as the books in today's Bible. There are a number of books written about many other scriptures that were eliminated by various councils in order to make up our standard Bible.[1]

The Bible is a collection of writings of some of the ancient prophets and was not intended to be all-inclusive. Some people quote one of the last verses of the Book of Revelation that says the book should not be added to. When John wrote that verse, there was no Bible. This verse had to pertain only to this particular revelation.

In fact, similar verses are found in Deuteronomy 4:2 and Proverbs 30:6.

Most scholars believe the apostle John wrote the Gospel of John as well as the Epistles of John after he wrote the Book of Revelation. The last verse of the Gospel of John, which, in fact, may be, chronologically, the last verse written in the current Bible states: "And there are also many other things which Jesus did, the which, if they should be written every one, I suppose that even the world itself could not contain the books that should be written" (John 21:25).

We are most fortunate today to have other sacred writings. In addition to the Bible we have the writings of the ancient prophets in the western he_____ lormon. We have the word of God a_____ets. One day we will have the word_____phets among the lost ten tribes of I_____iirds of The Book of Mormon, whic_____were not included in the Bible. "We_____rd of God as far as it is translated co_____), and I testify that we follow its teac_____ch on the earth.

Mary – this is my Dad

Here is a re_____n verifying the truthfulness of the Church.[2]

> I had an experience as a young man that I shall never forget. At college one day, some friends and I heard that Albert Einstein, the great scientist, was speaking to a faculty group. We attended the lecture and enjoyed his remarks very much. However, I didn't comprehend everything he said, but I did understand his concluding remark.
>
> He said, "Gentlemen, the deeper that I delve into the sciences of this universe, the more clearly I believe that one God or force or influence has organized all of it for our discovery."
>
> We walked quietly back to the dormitory and commenced discussing religion. There were five of us. Four of us belonged to different religions, and one was a professed atheist. One of the group was a brilliant fellow named Jim. He had a photographic mind. He could take a book, read the words on a page, close the book, and recite verbatim what he had read.
>
> When we started to discuss religion as a result of having heard Dr. Einstein's remarks, Jim went to the drawer of the dormitory and he took out a Bible. Then he went into the

hallway where he found a large chalkboard and maneuvered it into our room. Next, he took the Bible and went through it page by page. He was convinced that our Heavenly Father was and is a just God. He was convinced that in some of the 800 or so different beliefs and sects listed in the almanac that one represented the truth and the whole truth. He took a page of the Bible at a time and went to work on this chalkboard. It took him almost eight weeks; he had both sides of the chalkboard filled. Then he asked a secretary to come in, write down the information, summarize it, and type it on a five-by-seven card. Jim gave each of us a card and presented a plan to us. He said, "I have taken from the Bible all the evidences I could locate that would help a person identify the true Church. I'm convinced that Jesus Christ was sent here to organize his Church, and I believe that it is somewhere on the earth today."

So every Wednesday night and every Sunday, we went out looking for this Church. We visited the various churches, but none of them had what we were searching for. Some of the points that Jim had written down on our cards were that the true church would accept the scriptures; it would not have a paid ministry; it would have the proper authority from God; and it would claim to be the true church.

Not long after receiving the card, I decided to check out of school and train to become a paratrooper. While I was training, I had a wonderful experience I will share with you. I kept my five-by-seven card in my footlocker. On Sundays, I would occasionally attend one of the Protestant churches. As I would ride the bus to the outskirts of town to attend the church meetings, I noticed a group of fellows on board that I recognized as being in my class of paratrooper trainees. They would get off and go into a little brownstone church. They were a tremendous group. I never saw any of them with a cigarette in his mouth. I never heard a foul or obscene word or suggestive story from any of them. As I looked over their records, I noticed that they were all from the West. They were always laughing, having a tremendous time, and everyone liked them.

They had one young fellow, a little short farm boy from Utah, who seemed to be their leader. I was talking with him one day just as he was preparing to jump from their plane.

There had been a rather serious accident that morning with one of the trainees and I asked this farm boy how he felt about it.

"Oh, I don't mind," he said. "I know the answers to the three questions."

I thought, What's he talking about? I said, "What questions?"

And he said, "Unless you can answer three questions before you leave the earth, in great measure you have wasted your life."

About that time, the red light came on, and the little buzzer started sounding. I had to get ready to send him on his jump. All the time, I was wondering what on earth he was talking about.

The next evening I found out where he lived. As I walked into the barracks, he saw me coming and passed the word around. He was shining his boots. I walked up and said, "Hey, listen."

And he said, "What is it, Sarge?"

I said, "Tell me, what are these three questions?"

"Oh, don't you know? Well, number one, where did you come from before you came to earth?"

I thought, How silly can you be!

"Number two, why are you here? And number three, where are you going after you leave here?"

I said, "Anyone can answer. Wait a minute. I don't know. I don't know!"

Subsequently, I had other conversations with this young man and his companions. I had my five-by-seven card, and I asked them all the questions. As I progressed down through all the classifications of the true church, my heart beat harder. The church described by these men agreed with every single point on the card. I came to know for a surety that they were teaching me the truth and I joined The Church of Jesus Christ of Latter-day Saints.

A while later, I went through California on a furlough. The Church was having a conference at a stake center. As I walked in, I saw an Air Force captain. I looked again. It was Jim. He said, "What are you doing here?"

I said, "What are you doing here?"

He said, "This is my church."

I said, "Well, this is my church too!"

The thing I want to tell you is that all four of us who were left (one was killed in the war) armed with our five-by-seven cards found the same church. There might be some who would call this coincidental, but I know it wasn't.

While I was investigating the church, the young trainees pointed out from the scriptures that there would be another record that would be joined with the Bible. They showed me this other record.

I learned that gaining an understanding of the gospel was not a problem, only a process. The trainees said, "Don't take our word for it," when they handed me the new record, The Book of Mormon. They showed me a verse of scripture I will never forget: "And when ye shall receive these things, I would exhort you that ye would ask God, the Eternal Father, in the name of Christ, if these things are not true; and if ye shall ask with a sincere heart, with real intent, having faith in Christ, he will manifest the truth of it unto you, by the power of the Holy Ghost" (Moroni 10:4).

This impressed me. I didn't have to take anybody's word for it. I asked, and I received an answer. I know that this is the Church of Jesus Christ. I testify to you that the gospel is here upon the earth. I was looking for a church that had apostles, teachers, deacons and prophets. I found it. There's only one Church on the earth that has a Quorum of Twelve Apostles and that follows the Bible. I bear you my testimony that it is the truth and will bring you joy and that you will be able to bring this joy to other men. If you accept this truth, your entire family and posterity will rise up and call you blessed. I bear my testimony to you in the name of Jesus Christ, Amen.

Here are the seventeen points of the true church as presented by Floyd Weston. The following conditions, as specified in the Holy Scriptures, must exist for a church to qualify as the true church Jesus the Christ established when he was upon the earth.

1. **Will recognize the Holy Trinity as separate Persons.**
   A. Will know the identity of God (Father), Jesus Christ (Son), and the Holy Ghost (Spirit).
   B. Jesus Christ will be recognized as Head of the Church.
2. **Will accept the Holy Bible in its entirety** of which some parts of the record are missing.

3. **Will contain the same offices.**
    A. Twelve apostles are mandatory.
    B.Prophets, teachers, elders, evangelists, bishops, deacons, high priests, saints.
4. **Officers will be "Called of God."**
    A. College degree or license insufficient.
    B. Royal Priesthood.
    C. Can be married.
5. **Will have an unpaid Ministry.**
6. **Members will be workers in the Church.** Women included in activities.
7. **Baptism will be mandatory.**
    A. Probably by immersion.
    B. Must be authorized.
8. **Will believe in the Virgin Birth.**
9. **Will believe in literal resurrection.**
10. **Will honor Sunday as the Sabbath.**
11. **Will receive continuous revelation.**
12. **Will be payer of tithes.**
13. **Will partake of the Sacrament of the Lord.**
14. **Will believe in immortality and a heaven and a hell.**
15. **Will have miraculous occurrences,** healings, visions, tongues, prophecies.
16. **Will teach that Jesus Christ will come again.**
17. **Will be persecuted for beliefs.**

Notes:

1.   Crane, Frank, "Introduction to the Lost Books of the Bible," *The Lost Books of the Bible land the Forgotten Books of Eden*, World Bible Publishers, Alpha House, Inc., 1926 (note: no city provided).

2.   Weston, Floyd, *Seventeen Evidences of the True Church*, audio tape by Covenant Communications, Inc., American Fork, Utah, 1996.

3
The Dead Sea Scrolls
and Nag Hammadi Codices

Joseph Smith received the First Vision of God the Father and Jesus Christ in 1820. He learned later that he would be the Savior's instrument in restoring the ancient Church of Jesus Christ to the earth in these latter days. In 1827, an angel led Joseph to gold plates hidden in the ground. With divine help, Joseph translated the plates called The Book of Mormon. From the late 1820s to the early 1840s, Joseph received many revelations and translated additional ancient records. These are documented in modern-day scriptures called The Doctrine and Covenants and The Pearl of Great Price.

In The Book of Mormon, a prophet named Nephi wrote:

> *I beheld other books, which came forth by the power of the Lamb, from the Gentiles unto them, unto the convincing of the Gentiles and the remnant of the seed of my brethren, and also the Jews who were scattered upon all the face of the earth, that the records of the prophets and of the twelve apostles of the Lamb are true (1 Nephi 13:39).*

The Dead Sea Scrolls and the Nag Hammadi Codices are but a few of the documents that have already been discovered, which are evidence of the true Church. There are many more documents that have been discovered and will yet be discovered that provide and will provide even further evidence of the truth.

In early 1947, a small Bedouin tribe, called the Ta'amireh, was camped near the northwest shore of the Dead Sea not far from Jerusalem. One day, a fifteen-year-old goat herder named Mohammad-edh-Dhib noticed that a couple of the sheep or goats were missing. He began his search by looking in some of the numerous limestone caves in the area. He stopped at one cave and simply threw in a rock thinking that if any sheep or goats had climbed into the cave he could scare them out.[1]

The rock shattered something; the young goat herder was scared and ran away. The next day he returned with a friend and climbed into the cave. He saw that the rock had shattered a pottery jar that was filled with leather and papyrus scrolls. There was at least one other jar, which was also filled with scrolls.

A few months later, after some effort, the boys sold four of the scrolls in Bethlehem, which was about thirty-five miles away. The buyer was a boot maker named Kando, who bought them for use as shoe leather for the equivalent of approximately fourteen dollars. Kando was surprised when he unrolled the first scroll and was able to read the Book of Isaiah in Hebrew. He took the scrolls to the Syrian Orthodox archbishop, named Metropolitan Samuel, who bought them for $100. (These same four scrolls were sold a few years later for $250,000).[2] Samuel went to Eleazer Sukenik, an antiquities expert in Jerusalem, and showed him the scrolls.[3] Mr. Sukenik immediately recognized their value and importance.

Over the next few years, archeologists and historians searched hundreds of caves in the area and found eleven that contained scrolls, often in pottery jars as in the first cave. All or part of approximately 800 scrolls were found. Fewer than a dozen of them were intact. The rest were broken into about 25,000 fragments, many of which were no larger than a fingernail.[4] It all became a giant jigsaw puzzle,[5] which scholars have studied for the past fifty years trying to sort out nearly 800 separate documents with many or most of the pieces missing, and the remaining thousands of pieces resembling each other. Recently DNA testing has been used in an attempt to place similar pieces of the leather scrolls together.[6]

The scrolls, which were hidden by the people who lived in a city called Qumran, are now called the Dead Sea Scrolls. They have been dated using several different methods including Carbon 14, analyzing coins found in the jars, examining the handwriting of the scrolls, scrutinizing the pottery itself, and noting the emperors and leaders mentioned in them.[7] All this has determined that the scrolls were written between about 250 B.C. and 70 A.D.[8]

Approximately one fourth or about 200 of the scrolls are biblical,[9] meaning they are copies of the books of the Old Testament. There are, for example, fifteen copies of Genesis, seventeen of Exodus, thirteen of Leviticus, twenty-nine of Deuteronomy, twenty-one of Isaiah, thirty-six of Psalms, and so forth.[10] All of the books of the Old Testament are represented, except the Book of Esther. Perhaps this book was not found because it is small or because it does not contain the word "God." Ancient Jewish law forbade destroying any document containing the word "God."[11] None of the books of the New Testament are found among the scrolls for the simple reason that the people of Qumran were not Christian and the books of the

New Testament were written after the people of Qumran had been scattered by the Romans around 68-70 A.D.[12]

The scrolls have been deemed extremely important because of their age. Almost all modern-day Bibles have been translated from the Hebrew Masoretic text, the oldest of which is from about 900 A.D.; or from the Latin Vulgate text, the oldest of which is from about 405 A.D.; or from the Greek Septuagint text, the oldest of which is from about 360 A.D. Therefore, the Dead Sea Scrolls are 500 to 1,000 years older than the texts from which modern-day Bibles were translated.[13] In addition, until the discovery of the scrolls, very little was known about Jewish history between the period of Malachi (about 300 B.C.) and the birth of Christ.

It is estimated that less than five percent of the scrolls originally hidden at Qumran have been found.[14] This is based on analyzing the places in the caves where dozens of other jars must have been kept or on the words contained in some of the other scrolls. It is known that some scrolls were used during the cold winters by Arabs and nomads as firewood for hundreds of years. Some scholars think that many scrolls are still being held in bank vaults in Amman, Jordan.

Over the past forty years most of the scrolls and fragments have been translated. Only since 1991 have they been made available to the public in English and other languages.[15] Some of the scrolls are secular or non-religious. For example, the scroll originally called "The Manual of Discipline" and now called the "Rule of the Community" outlines strict rules that were in effect for the ancient Qumran community.[16] For example, if a member slept during a session of the community (like a church meeting), he was excommunicated or placed in penance for thirty days; if he spoke foolishly, he was in penance for three months; if he laughed foolishly, he was in penance for thirty days; or if he interrupted another person speaking, he was in penance for ten days.

Another interesting book is the copper scroll, which contains a list of buried gold and silver in the community. The current value of the treasure could be as much as $1 billion.[17] So far, that treasure has not been found. It is interesting that two thousand years ago, a group of religious people kept records engraved on metal, like The Book of Mormon. In addition to the biblical scrolls and the other secular scrolls, there are about 430 previously unknown books. Most of these are religious writings by prophets or others whose writings are not included in the Bible. Some of the interesting items in these books include the following:

Mahijah and Mahujah[18]

The Pearl of Great Price, translated by Joseph Smith, mentions a person named Mahijah who lived at the time of Enoch. "And there came a man unto him, whose name was Mahijah, and said unto him: Tell us plainly who thou art, and from whence thou comest?" (Moses 6:40). Mahijah is not found in the Bible. However, his name is mentioned several times in the Dead Sea Scrolls in the same period and in the same role as in *The Pearl of Great Price.* In one of the scrolls, Mahijah is forced to go to Enoch and ask who he really is. *The Pearl of Great Price* says: "As I was journeying and stood upon the place Mahujah . . ." (Moses 7:2). This name is also mentioned many times in the Scrolls, but not in the Bible.

Translation of Moses[19]

Moses wrote the first five books of the Bible, except for the last few verses of the Book of Deuteronomy as shown by the following verses. "So Moses the servant of the Lord died there in the land of Moab" (Deuteronomy 34:5). Verse seven says: "And Moses was an hundred and twenty years old when he died." However, from *The Book of Mormon* (Alma 45:19) and from modern-day prophets, we learn that Moses did not die. He was "translated," which means he was taken up by the Lord directly into heaven. To my knowledge, our Church is the only one to claim that Moses did not die but was translated. Among the Dead Sea Scrolls is a scroll called "The Ascension (or Assumption) of Moses," which speaks of this translation of Moses.

City of Enoch[20]

The Bible contains very little about the prophet Enoch (Genesis 5:18-24) and says nothing about the city named after him. However, *The Pearl of Great Price* states that the City of Enoch was translated, or taken up into heaven (Moses 7:69). The Dead Sea Scrolls describe in detail the translation of the City of Enoch.

The Vision of Enoch[21]

The Pearl of Great Price contains a marvelous description of the great vision given to Enoch, where he saw all things from the

beginning of the world to the end (Moses 7). None of this is found
in the Bible but a description of Enoch's wonderful vision is found
in the Scrolls.

Isaiah[22]

The Book of Mormon prophets frequently quoted Isaiah in their
writings. In fact, over one third of the Book of Isaiah is included in
The Book of Mormon. However, there are many variances between
The Book of Mormon verses of Isaiah and the biblical verses. One
scholar has found that eighty-nine of these variances in *The Book of
Mormon,* as compared to the *King James Version,* are indeed included in the versions of Isaiah as contained in the Dead Sea Scrolls or
in the other early versions of Isaiah, which include the Greek Septuagint, the Hebrew Masoretic or the Latin Vulgate.

Abraham[23]

The scrolls contain several stories about the prophet Abraham,
which are not found in the Bible, but are found in the Book of Abraham in *The Pearl of Great Price.* These include, for example, the
story about Abraham, his wife and the pharaoh.

Olive Tree[24]

The Book of Mormon contains a number of quotations from an
Old Testament prophet named Zenos, who is not mentioned in the
Bible. The longest quotation of Zenos is his beautiful allegory of the
olive tree (Jacob 5). The same allegory is in Hymn J (or 10) in the
Dead Sea Scrolls, whose author is not mentioned. It is also interesting to note that Hugh Nibley says this same allegory is contained in
an ancient document that was published in 1893. The author of that
allegory was translated as "Zenez."

Zenos[25]

The second longest quotation of Zenos in *The Book of Mormon*
is his hymn of thanksgiving and praise in Alma 33:3-11. A careful
reading of Hymn H (or 8) and Hymn J (or 10) of the "Thanksgiving
Hymns" in the Dead Sea Scrolls shows striking similarities with the
verses in Alma.

Joseph[26]

The scrolls contain numerous references to a future prophet
named "Asaph" who will restore the priesthood, commence the
great gathering, and be a forerunner to the Messiah in the last days.

He will face great opposition and be killed by lawless men. Asaph is translated into English as "Joseph."

The scrolls, as well as ancient Jewish traditions, contain many references to "Messiah-ben-Joseph" who is to precede "Messiah-ben-David" in the last days. "Messiah" means anointed one" and "ben" means "son of." This means that a prophet, descendant of Joseph of Egypt, will, in the latter days, precede the coming of the Savior, who was a descendant of David. A variant title of this prophet is "Messiah-ben-Ephraim." The scrolls mention that Messiah-ben-Joseph will restore true temple worship and bring to pass the restoration of the ten tribes.

In *The Book of Mormon,* we read of Joseph of Egypt's prophecies about the latter-day seer named Joseph who would descend from Joseph of Egypt (2 Nephi 3). We read of these same prophecies in Joseph Smith's translation of Genesis 50:33. Now we find similar prophecies about the latter-day prophet Joseph in the Dead Sea Scrolls.

Alma[27]

The name "Alma," which is in The Book of Mormon, is not in the Bible and was not known to be an ancient Israelite name, particularly as a masculine name ending in *a*. However, the name Alma appears in the scrolls and is spelled as in *The Book of Mormon*.[28]

Pre-Earth Life

The scrolls frequently mention a pre-earth life where all mankind lived as spirits with God the Father before coming to earth. To my knowledge, we are the only church on the earth that preaches this doctrine. It should be mentioned that the people of Qumran were living in a period of apostasy.[29] The fulness of the gospel was given to Heavenly Father's children at the beginning of each dispensation, that is to say, to Adam, Enoch, Noah, Abraham, Moses, and to Jesus Christ. After a period of time during each past dispensation, the people fell away and lost parts of the gospel. Although Qumran was in one of these periods of apostasy, it is interesting to see many of the doctrines, which they believed and taught, were remnants of the fulness they had lost.

Eternal Families[30]

The Scrolls have many references to eternal families and state that we will be sealed with our spouses and families in the hereafter.

They state that our families will be our greatest joy in the eternities. No other church besides ours teaches this today.

Eternal Progression[31]

The Scrolls clearly state that we can progress eternally, eventually becoming as God. Other churches have called us blasphemous when we teach this.

Priesthoods[32]

The Scrolls mention a greater and a lesser priesthood, essentially the same as the Melchizedek Priesthood and the Levitical or Aaronic Priesthood. Those called the "sons of Aaron" administered the temporal affairs of the community of Qumran.

Temples[33]

The Scrolls talk extensively about temples. The temple was the center of life for the community. The Scrolls mention the importance of a new name, key words, special garments, and an oath to keep the ceremony sacred, even at the peril of life itself.

Tithing[34]

The Scrolls frequently mention the importance of tithing as a commandment.

The Quorum of the Twelve and the Three[35]

The Scrolls say that the people of Qumran were led by twelve men of holiness" who were, in turn, led by three priests. This sounds like a high council and stake presidency. Under the twelve men of holiness were individuals called bishops who were descendants of Aaron and were common judges; they interviewed the people for worthiness, collected tithing, and administered communal goods.

Sacrament[36]

The Scrolls teach that the gospel was on earth from the beginning of time. It is interesting to note the Scrolls say that these people were led by twelve men and had a sacrament of bread and wine, 200 years before Christ was born.

Some Christian scholars have left their churches[37] after having studied the Scrolls because they show that the people of Qumran were practicing many of the principles of Christianity, such as the meaning of the Sacrament of the Last Supper, and the importance of the Twelve, even before Jesus Christ came to earth. Such scholars have said that their churches teach that Christianity did not begin before Christ.

We believe that the gospel was taught to Adam and has been given at the beginning of each dispensation to select groups since the beginning of time (Moses 5:58-59). Christ came as our Savior to pay for the transgression of Adam and to atone for the sins of all mankind. However, many Christian principles were revealed prior to his life on earth. For example, Joseph Smith's revision of the Book of Genesis says that Melchizedek served a sacrament of bread and wine to Abraham (JST Genesis 14:17).

Saints[38]

The people of Qumran called themselves "saints." A Catholic authority writing about the Scrolls said that the people of Qumran wrote so frequently about the future coming of the Messiah that they should be called Latter-day Saints." This authority said it was unfortunate that this name had already been taken.

Paradisiacal[39]

The Scrolls contain writings stating specifically that in the last days the earth will return to a state of innocence as before the Fall. This is similar to the Tenth Article of Faith, which states that we believe the earth will be renewed and receive its paradisiacal glory.

Spiritual Creation[40]

The Scrolls clearly mention the spiritual creation that preceded the temporal creation. In the scriptures this is taught only in *The Pearl of Great Price* (Moses 3:5).

War[41]

The War Scroll talks of the ongoing war between the sons of light and the sons of darkness. It says that God created both the Prince of Light and the Angel of Darkness. Many other churches have called us blasphemous when we teach that God is the father of Satan.

Prophets[42]

The Scrolls contain many writings that mention the importance of prophets on the earth at all times to direct us. No one else teaches this today.

The Imperfection of the Bible[43]

The Scrolls clearly prove that the Bible is not perfect but contains many errors of translation. This contradicts many Christian churches, which claim the Bible is word-for-word perfect.

The Bible Is Incomplete[44]

The Scrolls prove that there are many other books of scripture in addition to the Bible and that it is incomplete. This opposes the beliefs of most Christian churches, which hold that the Bible is complete.

Doctrines of Other Churches[45]

The Scrolls contain no mention of certain doctrines that are basic to many other Christian churches, such as the doctrine of "original sin," where all must pay for the transgression of Adam; a three-in-one Godhead, which is a spirit; a Eucharist or sacrament where the wafer and wine actually become the flesh and blood of Christ in the individual's mouth; or of baptism of infants and baptism by sprinkling. The fact is, the Dead Sea Scrolls specifically contradict these doctrines. For example, they state that baptism is by immersion, not for infants, and only after repentance from sins. They mention the "Glory of Adam,"[46] which is blasphemous to other churches.

The Nag Hammadi Codices

When the people of Palestine were scattered by the Romans in 68-70 A.D., some went north, some went east, and some went south to Egypt. Groups of Christians were formed. Those in the south called themselves Coptics and Gnostics.

In 1945, some men were digging in a cave near the Nile at a place called Nag Hammadi. They were looking for good soil for their farms. They found a cache of documents together in a large jar, which were in sorts of binders called codices. There were thirteen codices found, consisting of fifty-three books and about 1,000 total pages.

The documents have all been translated and are called the Nag Hammadi Codices. They have been dated to a period between 200 and 400 A.D. They were written by Gnostics who claimed to have superior knowledge to the northern or Roman Church, which was formed in 325 A.D. Some of the books found and translated include the Gospel of Thomas; the Gospel of Philip; the Apocalypse of James; the Apocalypse of Paul; the Apocrypha of John; the Acts of Peter; and the Epistle of Peter to Philip. It is important to remember that this was a period of apostasy, like the people of Qumran were in. However, it is interesting to observe the remnants of the truth in which the Gnostics still believed.

The Nag Hammadi Codices mention, among other things: Male and female gods;[47] a mirrored room called the "bridal chamber" where eternal marriage was performed;[48] the gospel of Philip says: "But the woman is united to her husband in the bridal chamber. Indeed those who have united in the bridal chamber will no longer be separated."[49]

The gospel was to be lost and then restored in the last days.[50] Ordinances may be performed for those who have died.[51] There was a Council in Heaven.[52] Ancient records would accompany the restoration of the gospel in the last days.[53] Adam was taught by three men in the Garden of Eden.[54] Ancient signs and oaths were given to those who were faithful in the Church and Jesus Christ gave a new name and key words to his apostles.[55]

The family remains together after death and the faithful will go on having sons and daughters in a "spiritual way" in the world to come.[56] Mankind can progress to become as God.[57] There are three levels in the hereafter.[58]

Do the Dead Sea Scrolls and the Nag Hammadi Codices prove that many of the key docrines of The Church of Jesus Christ of Latter-day Saints are true? In my mind, they do. In Nephi's great vision, he said:

I beheld other books, which came forth by the power of the Lamb, from the Gentiles unto them, unto the convincing of the Gentiles and the remnant of the seed of my brethren, and also the Jews who were scattered upon all the face of the earth, that the records of the prophets and of the twelve apostles of the Lamb are true (1 Nephi 13:39).

Charles A. Callis of the Council of the Twelve once said: "When Joseph Smith received the plates, he got down on his knees and said, 'O God, what will the world say?' and the voice of God came to him, 'Fear not. I will cause the earth to testify of the truth of these things.'"[59]

Notes:

1. Shanks, Hershel, *The Mystery and Meaning of the Dead Sea Scrolls*, Vintage Books, New York, 1998; p. 3.
2. Ibid. p. 19.
3. Ibid. p. 10.
4. Ibid. p. xiii-xiv. See also: *LDS Perspectives on the Dead Sea Scrolls*, Donald W. Parry and Dana M. Pike, Eds., FARMS, Provo, Utah, 1997; pp. 48, 197.
5. Pfeiffer, Charles E., *The Dead Sea Scrolls and the Bible*, Baker Book House, Grand Rapids, 1969; p. 17.
6. *LDS Perspectives on the Dead Sea Scrolls*, Donald W. Parry and Dana M. Pike, Eds., FARMS, Provo, Utah, 1997; pp. 191-205.
7. Mattson, Vernon W. Jr., *The Dead Sea Scrolls and Other Important Discoveries*, Buried Record Productions, Salt Lake City, 1988; p. 28. See also: Parry, Donald W. and Stephen D. Ricks, Eds., *The Dead Sea Scrolls: Questions and Responses for Latter-day Saints*, FARMS, Provo, Utah, 2000; pp. 10, 11.
8. *LDS Perspectives on the Dead Sea Scrolls*, Donald W. Parry and Dana M. Pike, Eds., FARMS, Provo, Utah, 1997; p. 47. See also: *Understanding the Dead Sea Scrolls*, Shanks, Hershel, Ed., Random House, N.Y., 1992; p. xix. See also: Ludlow, Daniel, "The Dead Sea Scrolls" audio tapes, Deseret Book Company, Salt Lake City, 1991.
9. Shanks, Hershel, *The Mystery and Meaning of the Dead Sea Scrolls*, Vintage Books, New York, 1998; pp. xiii, xv, 142. See also: *LDS Perspectives on the Dead Sea Scrolls*, Donald W. Parry and Dana M. Pike, Eds., FARMS, Provo, Utah, 1997; p. 48.
10. *LDS Perspectives on the Dead Sea Scrolls*, Donald W. Parry and Dana M. Pike, Eds., FARMS, Provo, Utah, 1997; p. 50.
11. *Understanding the Dead Sea Scrolls*, Shanks, Hershel, Ed., Random House, N.Y., 1992; p. xxi. See also: Ludlow, Daniel, "The Dead Sea Scrolls" tapes, Deseret Book Company, Salt Lake City, 1991.
12. *LDS Perspectives on the Dead Sea Scrolls*, Donald W. Parry and Dana M. Pike, Eds., FARMS, Provo, Utah, 1997; p. 52.
13. *LDS Perspectives on the Dead Sea Scrolls*, Donald W. Parry and Dana M. Pike, Eds., FARMS, Provo, Utah, 1997; p. 47. See also: Ludlow, Daniel, "The Dead Sea Scrolls After Thirty Years," course outline in the author's possession.

14. Shanks, Hershel, *The Mystery and Meaning of the Dead Sea Scrolls*, Vintage Books, New York, 1998; p. xvii.
15. Nibley, Hugh, "Teachings of The Book of Mormon," Lecture 10, Brigham Young University course outline in the author's possession.
16. Allegro, John, *The Dead Sea Scrolls: Reappraisal*, Penguin Books, London, 1964; p. 113.
17. Shanks, Hershel, *The Mystery and Meaning of the Dead Sea Scrolls,* Vintage Books, New York, 1998; pp. 180-196.
18. Nibley, Hugh, *Ancient Documents and The Pearl of Great Price*, transcript of 26 lectures on *The Pearl of Great Price,* Robert Smith and Robert Smythe, Eds., FARMS, Provo, Utah, 1986; p. 12. See also: Nibley, Hugh, *The Collected Works of Hugh Nibley,* Vol. 2, FARMS, Provo, Utah, 1988; pp. 277, 278. See also: Donald W. Parry, and Stephen D. Ricks, Eds., *The Dead Sea Scrolls: Questions and Responses for Latter-day Saints,* FARMS, Provo, Utah, 2000; p. 82.
19. Nibley, Hugh, *The Collected Works of Hugh Nibley*, Vol. 6, FARMS, Provo, Utah, 1988; pp. 174, 175. See also: Nibley, Hugh, *The Collected Works of Hugh Nibley,* Vol. 7, FARMS, Provo, Utah, 1988; pp. 286, 287. See also: Ludlow, Daniel, "The Dead Sea Scrolls" tapes, Deseret Book Company, Salt Lake City, 1991.
20. Nibley, Hugh, *The Collected Works of Hugh Nibley*, Vol. 2, FARMS, Provo, Utah, 1988; pp. 80, 81.
21. *Ibid.* pp. 243, 244.
22. Tvedtnes, John A., *Isaiah Variants in The Book of Mormon,* FARMS, Provo, Utah, 1984; p. 23.
23. Nibley, Hugh, "Teachings of The Book of Mormon," Lecture 10, Brigham Young University course outline in the author's possession.
24. Nibley, Hugh, *The Collected Works of Hugh Nibley,* Vol. 8, FARMS, Provo, Utah, 1988; pp. 326, 327. See also: Nibley, Hugh, *The Collected Works of Hugh Nibley*, Vol. 7, FARMS, Provo, Utah, 1988; pp. 283-287.
25. *Encyclopedia of Mormonism,* Daniel H. Ludlow, Ed., Vol. 4, (Zenos), Macmillan Publishing Company, New York, 1992; p. 1624.

26. Nibley, Hugh, *The Collected Works of Hugh Nibley*, Vol. 7, FARMS, Provo, Utah, 1988; p. 205. See also: *Isaiah and the Prophets: Inspired Voices from the Old Testament*, Religious Studies Monograph Series, Vol. 10, Religious Studies Center, Brigham Young University, Provo, Utah, 1984; pp. 13, 23-27. See also: McConkie, Joseph Fielding, *His Name Shall be Called Joseph*, Hawkes Publishing Inc., Salt Lake City, 1980; pp. 153-184. See also: Schonfield, Hugh J., *Secrets of Dead Sea Scrolls*, A.S. Barnes and Company, N.Y.; pp. 66-89.

27. *Ancient Scrolls from the Dead Sea*, Bradford, M. Gerald, Ed., FARMS, Provo, Utah, 1997; pp. 13, 14; See also: Hoskisson, Paul Y., "Alma as Hebrew Name," *Journal of Book of Mormon Studies*, Spring 1998; FARMS, Provo, Utah pp. 72, 73.

28. *LDS Perspectives on the Dead Sea Scrolls*, Donald W. Parry and Dana M. Pike, Eds., FARMS, Provo, Utah, 1997; pp. 76, 77. See also: Mattson, Vernon W. Jr., *The Dead Sea Scrolls and Other Important Discoveries*, Buried Record Productions, Salt Lake City, 1988; p. 111. See also: Seaich, Eugene, *Mormonism, the Dead Sea Scrolls and the Nag Hammadi Texts*, Sounds of Zion, Midvale, Utah, 1980; p. 13. See also: Ludlow, Daniel, "The Dead Sea Scrolls" tapes, Deseret Book Company, Salt Lake City, 1991.

29. Mattson, Vernon W. Jr., *The Dead Sea Scrolls and Other Important Discoveries*, Buried Record Productions, Salt Lake City, 1988; p. 21. See also: Ludlow, Daniel, "The Dead Sea Scrolls" tapes, Deseret Book Company, Salt Lake City, 1991.

30. Nibley, Hugh, "Teachings of The Book of Mormon," Lecture 10, p. 12, Brigham Young University course outline in the author's possession.

31. Ludlow, Daniel, "The Dead Sea Scrolls" tapes, Deseret Book Company, Salt Lake City, 1991.

32. Nibley, Hugh, "Teachings of The Book of Mormon," Lecture 10, p. 9, Brigham Young University course outline in the author's possession. See also: Ludlow, Daniel, "The Dead Sea Scrolls" tapes, Deseret Book Company, Salt Lake City, 1991. See also: Mattson, Vernon W. Jr., *The Dead Sea Scrolls and Other Important Discoveries*, Buried Record Productions, Salt Lake City, 1988; p. 105.

33. *LDS Perspectives on the Dead Sea Scrolls*, Donald W. Parry and Dana M. Pike, Eds., FARMS, Provo, Utah, 1997, pp. 35, 184, 185. See also: Ludlow, Daniel, "The Dead Sea Scrolls" tapes,

Deseret Book Company, Salt Lake City, 1991. See also: Blake Ostler, *BYU Studies,* Vol. 22, No. 1, Brigham Young University, Provo, Utah; p. 37.

34. Nibley, Hugh, "Teachings of The Book of Mormon," Lecture 10, p. 1, Brigham Young University course outline in the author's possession. See also: Ludlow, Daniel, "The Dead Sea Scrolls" tapes, Deseret Book Company, Salt Lake City, 1991.

35. Mattson, Vernon W. Jr., *The Dead Sea Scrolls and Other Important Discoveries,* Buried Record Productions, Salt Lake City, 1988; pp. 22, 105. See also: *LDS Perspectives on the Dead Sea Scrolls,* Donald W. Parry and Dana M. Pike, Eds., FARMS, Provo, Utah, 1997; pp. 33, 184. See also: Seaich, Eugene, *Mormonism, the Dead Sea Scrolls and the Nag Hammadi Texts,* Sounds of Zion, Midvale, Utah, 1980; p. 42. See also: Ludlow, Daniel, "The Dead Sea Scrolls" tapes, Deseret Book Company, Salt Lake City, 1991.

36. *LDS Perspectives on the Dead Sea Scrolls,* Donald W. Parry and Dana M. Pike, Eds., FARMS, Provo, Utah, 1997; p. 106. See also: Mattson, Vernon W. Jr., *The Dead Sea Scrolls and Other Important Discoveries,* Buried Record Productions, Salt Lake City, 1988; pp. 22, 103.

37. Nibley, Hugh, *The Collected Works of Hugh Nibley*, Vol. 7, FARMS, Provo, Utah, 1988; p. 21. See also: Nibley, Hugh, "Teachings of The Book of Mormon," Lecture 10, p. 9, Brigham Young University course outline in the author's possession.

38. Ludlow, Daniel, "The Dead Sea Scrolls" tapes, Deseret Book Company, Salt Lake City, 1991.

39. Mattson, Vernon W. Jr., *The Dead Sea Scrolls and Other Important Discoveries,* Buried Record Productions, Salt Lake City, 1988; pp. 122, 123.

40. *LDS Perspectives on the Dead Sea Scrolls,* Donald W. Parry and Dana M. Pike, Eds., FARMS, Provo, Utah, 1997; p. 81.

41. *Ibid.* pp. 79, 84. See also: Pfeiffer, Charles F., *The Dead Sea Scrolls and the Bible,* Baker Book House, Grand Rapids; p. 137. See also: Ludlow, Daniel, "The Dead Sea Scrolls After Thirty Years," course outline in the author's possession. See also: Shanks, Hershel, *The Mystery and Meaning of the Dead Sea Scrolls*, Vintage Books, New York, 1998; p. 76.

42. Seaich, Eugene, *Mormonism, the Dead Sea Scrolls and the Nag Hammadi Texts*, Sounds of Zion, Midvale, Utah, 1980; p. 43. See also: Ludlow, Daniel, "The Dead Sea Scrolls" tapes, Deseret

Book Company, Salt Lake City, 1991. See also: *Encyclopedia of Mormonism (Dead Sea Scrolls)*, Daniel H. Ludlow, Ed., Macmillan Publishing Company, New York, 1992; p. 363.

43. *LDS Perspectives on the Dead Sea Scrolls*, Donald W. Parry and Dana M. Pike, Eds., FARMS, Provo, Utah, 1997; p. 54-62. See also: Ludlow, Daniel, "The Dead Sea Scrolls After Thirty Years," course outline in the author's possession.

44. *Encyclopedia of Mormonism (Dead Sea Scrolls)*, Daniel H. Ludlow, Ed., Macmillan Publishing Company, New York, 1992; p. 363.

45. Mattson, Vernon W. Jr., *The Dead Sea Scrolls and Other Important Discoveries*, Buried Record Productions, Salt Lake City, 1988; p. 113. See also: Ludlow, Daniel, "The Dead Sea Scrolls" tapes, Deseret Book Company, Salt Lake City, 1991. See also: Shanks, Hershel, *The Mystery and Meaning of the Dead Sea Scrolls*, Vintage Books, New York, 1998; p. 78. See also: Nibley, Hugh, "Teachings of The Book of Mormon," Lecture 10, p. 12, Brigham Young University course outline in the author's possession.

46. Nibley, Hugh, "Teachings of The Book of Mormon," Lecture 10, Brigham Young University course outline in the author's possession.

47. Mattson, Vernon W. Jr., *The Dead Sea Scrolls and Other Important Discoveries*, Buried Record Productions, Salt Lake City, 1988; p. 41.

48. *Ibid.* p. 41. See also: Seaich, Eugene, *Mormonism, the Dead Sea Scrolls and the Nag Hammadi Texts*, Sounds of Zion, Midvale, Utah, 1980; pp. 80, 129.

49. *The Nag Hammadi Library*, Robinson, James M. Harper, Ed., San Francisco, 1990; p. 151.

50. Mattson, Vernon W. Jr., *The Dead Sea Scrolls and Other Important Discoveries*, Buried Record Productions, Salt Lake City, 1988; p. 41.

51. *Ibid.* p. 41.

52. Seaich, Eugene, Mormonism, the Dead Sea Scrolls and the Nag Hammadi Texts, Sounds of Zion, Midvale, Utah, 1980; p. 130.

53. Mattson, Vernon W. Jr., *The Dead Sea Scrolls and Other Important Discoveries*, Buried Record Productions, Salt Lake City, 1988; p. 41.

54. *Ibid.* p. 41.

55. *Ibid.* pp. 41, 130.

56. *Ibid.* p. 42

57. *Ibid.* p. 42. See also: Seaich, Eugene, *Mormonism, the Dead Sea Scrolls and the Nag Hammadi Texts*, Sounds of Zion, Midvale, Utah, 1980; p. 113.

58. Seaich, Eugene, *Mormonism, the Dead Sea Scrolls and the Nag Hammadi Texts*, Sounds of Zion, Midvale, Utah, 1980; pp. 110, 111.

59. Richards, LeGrand, *Conference Report,* The Church of Jesus Christ of Latter-day Saints, Salt Lake City, October 1946; p. 126.

4
Apostasy and Restoration

The Church of Jesus Christ of Latter-day Saints is the same church that Jesus Christ organized during his life on the earth. Paul described a saint as a disciple of Christ and a member of the Church. The term "latter-day" simply distinguishes the current Church from the original Church. The Church is not Catholic, nor Protestant, nor is it a sect. Rather, it is the restored Church of Jesus Christ.

The Bible says everything the ancient prophets taught from the time the world began must be restored before Christ comes again (Acts 3:19-21). In order to restore something, it must first be lost. Therefore, everything in the Church at the time of Christ must first be lost or removed from the earth and then later restored.

The greatest day in history was the Sunday that the Savior was resurrected. Many scholars believe this was April 5, 34 A.D.[1] Jesus Christ, the Savior of the world, had been crucified the previous Friday and his body laid in a tomb with the entrance covered by a large stone and guarded by Roman soldiers. Early that Sunday morning Mary Magdalene and another woman named Mary went to visit the tomb. They were astonished to see that the soldiers were gone and the stone had been rolled aside. Then they beheld an angel who said: "Fear not ye for I know that ye seek Jesus, which was crucified. He is not here for he is risen" (Matthew 28:5, 6).

The risen Savior then appeared and spoke first to Mary Magdalene in the garden by the sepulcher (Mark 16:9; John 20:11-18). This was certainly the most glorious day from the time of the creation of the earth, as it ensured that all would be resurrected and have the opportunity to return to our Heavenly Father. As described in the Bible, the risen Christ then appeared to many others. He appeared once more to Mary Magdalene and the other Mary (Matthew 28:9). He appeared to ten of the apostles (John 20:19). He appeared to all eleven apostles at least four times: While they were eating (Mark 16:14; John 20:26); at the Sea of Tiberias (John 21:1-24); on a mountain in Galilee (Matthew 28:16, 17); and when he ascended into heaven (Acts 1).

Christ appeared to two men on the road to Emmaus (Luke 24: 13-15, 18). He appeared to 500 people at one time (1 Corinthians 15:5-8). Stephen saw him standing on the right hand of God (Acts 7:56). He appeared to Paul (Acts 23:11; 26:16). He appeared to Peter (Luke 24:34). He appeared to James (1 Corinthians 15:7), and he appeared to John (Revelations 1:17).

As the Gospel of Jesus Christ spread throughout the known world, branches or units of his Church were organized. The apostles traveled among the branches and, by revelation, called local leaders, such as bishops, to ensure the doctrine of the Church of Jesus Christ remained pure. They answered the many questions and resolved many issues that would inevitably arise among the Saints. Branches of the Church included Antioch, Ephesus, Corinth, Athens, Thessalonica, Jerusalem, and others.

The Savior organized the Church on a foundation of twelve apostles (Ephesians 2:20). When he called them he said, "Ye have not chosen me, but I have chosen you, and ordained you" (John 15:16). He also declared through Paul that there should be twelve apostles in the Church until all people came to a "unity of the faith" (Ephesians 4:11-13). The world has never yet come to a unity of the faith, so it is evident that we still need apostles in the true Church of Jesus Christ.

It is clear that the apostles knew they should continue the Quorum of the Twelve. They chose Matthias as the replacement for Judas Iscariot (Acts 1:23-26). In addition to Matthias there were at least three other apostles chosen: Paul (Romans 1:1); Barnabus (1 Corinthians 9:5, 6); and James, the brother of Christ (Galatians 1:19).

As the apostles died within a short period of time without being replaced there was no one to travel to the individual church units to select bishops and to resolve Church issues.[2] There was no one to keep the doctrine in check. There would have certainly been many questions arise, such as: How can you immerse a dying man who wants to be baptized? At what age may one be baptized? Is baptism not required for everyone? When John said, "God is Spirit" (John 4:24), what did he mean? What did Jesus mean when he said that anyone who had seen him had seen the Father (John 14:9)? When Christ said that He is One with the Father (John 17:21, 22), what did he mean?

The individual branches of the church had no alternative but to select their own local leaders, such as bishops, and to determine church doctrine by consensus or by voting. There was no central direction of the churches of any kind.

Over 300 years, much of the truth as taught by the Savior was lost, just as it had been prophesied by Isaiah who said that darkness was to cover the earth (Isaiah 60:2), and the earth was to be defiled (Isaiah 24:5). There was to be a famine of words of the Lord and the words would not to be found (Amos 8:11, 12). There would be false teachers among the Saints (2 Peter 2:1) and false prophets (1 John 4:1). A falling away before the Second Coming of Christ would take place (2 Thessalonians 2:3). (In the original writings mention is made of *the* Apostasy, not *an* Apostasy.[3])

There were wolves among the Saints (Acts 20:29), and perilous times (2 Timothy 3:1-3) in which sound doctrine would not endure (2 Timothy 4:3). There would be false Christs and many false prophets who would deceive many, even the elect (Matthew 24:5, 24).

Other scriptures state that no man on earth should be called "father" (Matthew 23:9), that saints should beware of scribes in long robes (Mark 12:38), and men of the Church should not be forbidden to marry and not to abstain from eating meats (1 Timothy 4:1-4).

There was significant division among the individual churches.[4] Groups called Coptics and Gnostics were organized in Egypt. Mandeans were organized in what is now Iraq and Iran. Some of the northern groups became organized in what is now Turkey, Greece and Italy and followed the teachings of a bishop named Arius. Others followed the teachings of another bishop named Athanasius.[5]

In 325 A.D., Constantine observed great divisions among the Christian churches in his Roman Empire.[6] He did not become a Christian until he was baptized by sprinkling on his deathbed.[7] He was indeed a wicked ruler who killed his wife, his son, his brother-in-law and his nephew.[8] His mother, who was a Christian, was the first to begin searching for Church relics, such as the Savior's cross. Since 300 years had passed since the death of Jesus Christ, it is highly unlikely that she found any true relics.[9]

Constantine wanted the churches to be united in order to avoid contention and disputations in the empire. He convened a council in which representatives of each local church were to meet in Nicea (anciently in Turkey). In the Council of Nicea, representatives voted on the nature of God—whether he had a body or was a Spirit. They also voted as to whether he was one God or three Gods in one. The Roman Catholic Church was first organized during this council.[10]

Representatives wrote the Nicene Creed at this council. Today many religions and people quote this creed or a subsequent version of it called the Athanasian Creed. It states:

We worship one God in Trinity, and Trinity in Unity, neither confounding the persons, nor dividing the substance. For there is one person of the Father, another of the Son, and another of the Holy Ghost. But the Godhead of the Father, Son and Holy Ghost, is all one: the glory equal, the majesty co-eternal. Such as the Father is, such is the Son; and such is the Holy Ghost. The Father uncreate, the Son uncreate and the Holy Ghost uncreate. The Father incomprehensible, the Son incomprehensible and the Holy Ghost incomprehensible. The Father eternal, the Son eternal, and the Holy Ghost eternal. And yet there are not three eternals; but one eternal. As also there are not three incomprehensibles, nor three uncreated; but one uncreated, and one incomprehensible. So likewise the Father is Almighty, the Son Almighty, and the Holy Ghost Almighty, and yet there are not three Almighties, but one Almighty. So the Father is God, the Son is God, and the Holy Ghost is God, and yet there are not three Gods but one God.[11]

Over the next few years after the council was held, the first Bible was compiled in an attempt to help unify the various branches of the church. It consisted of a compilation of some of the many religious books that had been written by prophets for more than 2,000 years. The first Bible, including the New Testament, was compiled in 367 A.D. The word "bible" comes from the Greek word *biblia*, which means "books" or "collection of books."[12]

Many quote one of the last verses of the present-day Bible as so-called "proof" that it was complete and that no new scriptures should ever be added. This verse says, "If any man shall add unto these things, God shall add unto him the plagues that are written in this book" (Revelation 22:18). In view of the fact that in The Church of Jesus Christ of Latter-day Saints we believe that there are additional holy scriptures which are also the word of God, how do we explain the fact that the Bible seems to say God would not allow any more scripture to be added?

The Book of Revelation was written around 100 A.D.; the Bible was not compiled until 367 A.D. Therefore, the verse in question could not apply to the whole Bible; rather, it applies only to the Book of Revelation, since further scripture was written *after* the Book of Revelation. Statements similar to Revelation 22:18 are found Deuteronomy 4:2 and in Proverbs 30:6. Obviously these statements in the Old Testament could not apply to the whole Bible. If they did, that would mean that the entire New Testament and several books of the Old Testament, too, would not be the word of the Lord.

The apostle John was the author of the Book of Revelation. He also wrote the Gospel of John and three epistles *after* he wrote the Book of Revelation.[13] It would appear that the actual last verse of the Bible is the last verse of the Book of John, which states that the world could not contain the books that should be written about Jesus Christ (John 21:25).

The Bible mentions several other books and says that they, too, are scripture. However, they are not part of today's Bible. They include such writings as the Book of the Covenant (Exodus 24:7; 2 Kings 23:2, 21), the Book of the Wars of the Lord (Numbers 21:14), the Book of Nathan the Prophet (2 Chronicles 8:29), the Book of Enoch (Jude 1:14), and others.[14] It, therefore, becomes clear that Revelation 22:18 is talking about that particular book, not other books and not the New Testament itself nor the Bible as a whole.

The Apostasy, which had been prophesied, continued over several centuries. It included the evil acts of men, of course, but it also had to do with the doctrine and the organization of the church. For example: the doctrine of "original sin," (the belief that man must pay for the transgression of Adam) was conceived by Augustine in the fifth century. It was based on a mistranslation of a verse in the Book of Romans (5:12). Augustine thought we had all sinned in Adam.[15] The idea of original sin denies the Atonement of Christ where he paid for the transgression of Adam. Paul said, "For as in Adam all die, even so in Christ shall all be made alive" (1 Corinthians 15:21, 22).

The crucifix did not become part of the church until the sixth century.[16] In the seventh century the church began to teach the doctrine of transubstantiation, which means that the wafer used in the Eucharist becomes the actual flesh of Christ and the wine becomes his actual blood.[17] Clovis, the first king of France, was baptized by immersion in the city of Rheims in 496 A.D. The monarchs who followed Clovis were also baptized by immersion in the same font, which exists even today under the Rheims cathedral. Members of the church were baptized by immersion up until the eighth century, then the ordinance was changed to just sprinkling.

Around 1000 A.D. the Crusades were organized by the church as a means to attempt to free the Holy Land from the Muslims. There were ten Crusades, which all failed.[19] Millions of innocent people were massacred. To induce Christians to go on the Crusades, the church promised them forgiveness of all their sins. It was at this time that indulgences came into existence wherein forgiveness of even future sins was granted for a price.[20] This meant, for example, that men could pay for an indulgence and be forgiven in advance for all their rapes, murders, plundering, and pillaging while fighting in the Crusades.

Baptism of infants began 500 years after the death of Christ but was not universal until the thirteenth century.[21] The doctrines of papal infallibility and of no revelation by the pope were not decided until the nineteenth century.[22] Although the Catholic Church admits that many popes throughout history made many errors (e.g., Galileo and Copernicus were excommunicated for claiming the earth was not the center of the universe and that the earth revolved around the sun), and that there were many very wicked popes, the Catholic Church declared by the vote of cardinals in 1870 that popes were infallible and always had been.[23] In addition, they decided by vote that popes do not receive revelation; rather, they interpret the Bible by inspiration.

In March 2000, Pope John Paul II apologized for the past wrongs of the Catholic Church. It was generally reported by the press that Pope John Paul II was referring to the Church's not having done anything to denounce the Holocaust, the atrocities of the Crusades and the Inquisition, and several other such tragedies. It is difficult to reconcile John Paul's apology and these past weaknesses with the doctrine of infallibility. It's strange that somehow the pope is infallible, yet he (they) make such extreme mistakes in judgment. Then, also, how can one be infallible and not receive revelation. Or, how can one not receive revelation but be infallible?

The Apostasy does not negate the fact that there were many good and righteous people on the earth. It may also be said that there were many good church leaders who tried to lead the people in righteous ways. Nevertheless, as the Bible clearly prophesied, after the death of the Savior, the Apostasy would occur as the result of evil that crept into the Church. The Gospel was indeed taken from the earth as the leaders died and the authority to act in the name of the Lord through his priesthood power, died also.

The Catholic Church was organized by Constantine, a non-Christian. The bishop of Rome became known as the pope, as a result of political maneuvering and exercise of influence. The bishop of Rome was not even in attendance at the Council of Nicea and was viewed at the time as being no more or less than equal to the other 1,800 bishops in the Roman Empire. [24, 25] Up to 869 A.D., not one of the first eight councils of the Roman church was called by the bishop of Rome.[26] His was a minor role, not recognized as having any authority over the Catholic Church for many centuries.[27]

Between 300 and 400 A.D., however, the bishop of Rome began claiming significant authority.[28] Lists of previous bishops were compiled, supposedly indicating a line back to the apostle Peter, who died 300 years earlier.[29] Today there exists more than one list of popes, although there is no evidence that Peter was ever the bishop of Rome. Indeed, the leaders of the Church, as established and organized by the Savior, set at the head of the Church the Quorum of Twelve Apostles. Bishops were called as leaders of individual branches or units. They were to lead the Church on a local level. Peter was the chief apostle, not a bishop.

Lists complied by the Catholic Church list Peter, who was martyred around 65 A.D., followed by Linus appointed in 65 A.D., Cletus in 79 A.D., and Clement in 90 A.D. These men, it appears, were undoubtedly faithful Christians. But lest we forget, the apostle John wrote the Book of Revelation around 100 A.D. If Linus, Cletus and Clement were indeed the heads of Christ's Church, why was the Book of Revelation revealed through John and not one of them?[30] If they were so significant to the Church, why did John not mention any of the three of them in his Book of Revelation, the Book of John or in any of his three epistles, all of which were written between 92 A.D. and 105 A.D.? There is no evidence that any of these men ever had apostolic authority as did John.

The Catholic Church tries to establish its line of priesthood authority by referring to Christ's words when he said, "Thou art Peter and upon this rock I will build my Church" (Matthew 16:18). However, the word "Peter" is masculine (Petros), and the word for rock in both Latin and Greek is feminine (Petra). It is apparent that Christ could not have meant that Peter was the rock. It would have been like saying "Thou art 'X' and upon this 'Y' I will build my church."[31]

In the French Bible, there is a footnote to Matthew 16:18 explaining that the phrase "upon this rock" refers to 1 Corinthians 3:11, which says: "For other foundation can no man lay than that is laid, which is Jesus Christ." First Corinthians 10:4 says, "For they drank of that spiritual Rock that followed them: and that Rock was Christ." Ephesians 2:20 says, ". . . Jesus Christ being the chief cornerstone."

The recent Catholic Bibles eliminate all footnote references to Peter being the "rock."[32] The complete scripture in Matthew 16:15-19 states that when Peter said Christ was the Son of the living God, Jesus responded that, "Flesh and blood hath not revealed it unto thee, but my Father which is in Heaven . . . and upon this rock I will build my church." He clearly meant the rock of revelation or the rock of Christ.[33]

For hundreds of years bishops, popes, and other church leaders were chosen by strong political leaders, such as emperors. For example: in the 800s A.D., Charlemagne freely chose and eliminated bishops. He exiled church leaders who disagreed with him.[34] This was also done by monarchs in England, Spain, Germany, and elsewhere.

There was no single, recognized leader of the Catholic Church for many hundreds of years.[35] In 1054 A.D. the church was split in half when some wanted Constantinople to be the headquarters of the church and others wanted Rome.[36] The title of pope was not reserved for the bishop of Rome until the eleventh century.[37] In 1409 there were three popes and there were a number of gaps of time when there was no pope at all.[38] There were some popes who were children.[39] Some popes were very wicked men.[40]

Between 1200 and 1300 A.D., the European Inquisition took place, in which non-Catholics in Spain, France, and in other countries were murdered.[41] John Huss tried to reform the church in the 1400s and was burned at the stake.[42] These were truly the Dark Ages.

The Lord then began preparing the world for the Restoration of all things as had been prophesied in the scriptures. All things taught by the prophets since the beginning of the world had to be restored before the Second Coming of Christ (Acts 3:19-21). If something is to be restored, it must first have been taken away.

Some of the other scriptures pertaining to the Restoration include: The Lord said Zion would be established in the tops of the mountains (Isaiah 2:1-3). In the last days, the house of the Lord would be established in the tops of the mountains and people would flow unto it (Micah 4:1, 2). The scriptures also say Elijah would come (Malachi 4:5). Elias would restore all things (Matthew 17:11). The dispensation of the fullness of times would come about (Ephesians 1:10). The stone (Gospel) would roll forth to fill the whole earth (Daniel 2:35, 45). An angel with the everlasting gospel will come (Revelation 14:6, 7).

The Restoration of all things did indeed come as the result of a number of significant events. In 1455, which could be called the *first event,* the printing press was invented by Johannes Gutenberg and the Bible was printed for the first time with movable type. However, for more than 400 years following this invention, the Bible was only available to the clergy (up until about seventy-five years ago in the Catholic Church). The printing of the Bible made it possible, however, for the Catholic clergy to compare their church doctrines to the scriptures. This brought about the Reformation.

The *second event* occurred in 1492 with the discovery of the New World by Christopher Columbus.

The Book of Mormon states:

And I looked and beheld a man among the Gentiles, who was separated from the seed of my brethren by the many waters; and I beheld the Spirit of God, that it came down and wrought upon the man; and he went forth upon the many waters, even unto the seed of my brethren, who were in the promised land (1 Nephi 13:12).

James E. Talmage quoted Columbus, then commented:

"Who can doubt that this fire was not merely mine, but also of the Holy Spirit who encouraged me with the radiance of marvelous illumination from his sacred Holy Scriptures, by a most clear and powerful testimony . . . urging me to press forward? Continually, without a moment's hesitation, the Scriptures urged me to press forward with great haste."

Columbus not only believed the Lord inspired him on his first voyage, but was also convinced that the Holy Scriptures prophesied of his great enterprise. During the last years of his life he was working on a manuscript called Book of Prophecies which included a collection of prophetic passages, especially from Isaiah, which he believed pertained to his expedition.[43]

The ***third event*** took place in the 1500s, which was the Reformation. In 1517 Luther posted his ninety-five theses on the door of the Catholic Church. This was the beginning of the Lutheran Church. King Henry VIII began the Church of England, also called the Episcopal or Anglican Church, in 1534. John Calvin began the Presbyterian Church in 1540. Since these individuals protested the teachings of the Catholic Church, the organizations they founded were called "Protestant" churches.

Many of these individuals were led by the Spirit and they took the Restoration of the Gospel as far as they were able. Many of them knew, however, that they could not complete the Restoration. For example, Martin Luther said: "I have sought nothing beyond reforming the Church in conformity with the Holy Scriptures. The spiritual powers have been not only corrupted by sin, but absolutely destroyed. I say that Christianity has ceased to exist."[44]

John Wesley, founder of the Methodist Church, said, "It does not appear that these extraordinary gifts of the Holy Ghost were common in the Church for more than two or three centuries. The Christians had no more of the Spirit of Christ than the other heathens. The Christians had only a dead form left."[45]

Roger Williams, pastor of the oldest Baptist church in America, resigned his position in 1600 stating that: "There was no regularly constituted church on earth, nor any person authorized to administer any Church ordinance, nor can there be until new apostles are sent by the Great Head of the Church for whose coming I am seeking."[46]

During the 1600s and 1700s, the ***fourth event*** took place: The colonization of America.[47] In Europe significant persecution of those who tried to worship as they wished was occurring. The only place true freedom could be found was the New World. Over the next 200 years the Americas were colonized by the Pilgrims and the Puritans and others who sought, among other things, freedom of religion. *The Book of Mormon* states: "And it came to pass that I beheld the Spirit of God, that it wrought upon other Gentiles; and they went forth out of captivity, upon the many waters" (1 Nephi 13:13).

The *fifth event* was **the establishment and organization of a free country.** In 1776 the Declaration of Independence was written and in 1789 the Constitution was ratified by the states. These guaranteed freedom of religion. The founders of the United States felt directed by the Lord throughout their proceedings.[48] This was the first country in the world where freedom of religion was officially sanctioned. The world was finally prepared for the Restoration of the Gospel of Jesus Christ, as had been promised and prophesied in the scriptures.

On a spring morning in 1820, the **sixth event** began; **the restoration of the true Church of Jesus Christ.** This was the second greatest day in the history of the world. A young man named Joseph Smith wanted to know if the true church of God was on the earth and, if so, which church it was. He lived with his family in the small town of Palmyra in upper New York state where every church was proclaiming to be the one and only true church.

He read in the Bible (James 1:5) that if one lacked wisdom, he should ask God who would give him the answer. It should be noted that a century earlier, on any other continent, Joseph would have been burned at the stake for merely reading the Bible.[49] By 1820, however, the Lord had prepared the earth for the Restoration of the Gospel.

On that particular morning in 1820, Joseph went into a grove of trees not far from the family's farm. He knelt down and prayed with all his might that he might know which church he should join. Later, he wrote about his experience:

> I saw a pillar of light exactly over my head, above the brightness of the sun, which descended gradually until it fell upon me. When the light rested upon me, I saw two personages whose brightness and glory defy all description, standing above me in the air. One of them spake unto me by name and said, pointing to the other, "This is My Beloved Son. Hear Him!" (*Joseph Smith History* 1:16, 17).

Over the next few years the fulness of the Gospel was restored to the earth, including the original doctrines, organization, and priesthood authority of the original Church of Jesus Christ which the Savior established during his earthly mission. Truly, the two greatest days in the history of mankind are the day the Savior resurrected from the dead, and the day in 1820 when he commenced to restore his true Church to the earth.

Notes:

1. Lefgren, John C., *April Sixth,* Deseret Book, Salt Lake City, 1980; p. 47.
2. Barker, James L., *Apostasy from the Divine Church*, Deseret News Press, Salt Lake City, 1960; pp. 137-148; 202; 532.
3. *Church News,* The Church of Jesus Christ of Latter-day Saints, Salt Lake City, November 25, 1995; p. 5.
4. Barker, James L., *Apostasy from the Divine Church*, Deseret News Press, Salt Lake City, 1960; pp. 151; 245, 254.
5. Petersen, Mark E., *The Great Prologue,* Deseret Book, Salt Lake City, 1975; pp. 19, 20. See also: Barker, James L., *Apostasy from the Divine Church*, Deseret News Press, Salt Lake City, 1960; pp. 238-244.
6. Barker, James L., *Apostasy from the Divine Church*, Deseret News Press, Salt Lake City, 1960; pp. 151; 245-254.
7. Petersen, Mark E., *The Great Prologue,* Deseret Book, Salt Lake City, 1975; p. 21.
8. Barker, James L., *Apostasy from the Divine Church*, Deseret News Press, Salt Lake City, 1960; p. 277.
9. *Ibid.* p. 540.
10. Miller, Lee, "Commandments of Men," *The Instructor,* The Church of Jesus Christ of Latter-day Saints, Salt Lake City, April 1964; inside back cover. See also: Barker, James L., *Apostasy from the Divine Church*, Deseret News Press, Salt Lake City, 1960; pp. 249-271. Talmage, James E., *The Great Apostasy*, Deseret Book, Salt Lake City, 1968; p. 104.
11. Bible Dictionary, The Church of Jesus Christ of Latter-day Saints, Salt Lake City, 1979; p. 62.
12. Barker, James L., *Apostasy from the Divine Church,* Deseret News Press, Salt Lake City, 1960; p. 8.
13. Topical Guide; scriptures, lost," The Church of Jesus Christ of Latter-day Saints, Salt Lake City, 1979.
14 Barker, James L., *Apostasy from the Divine Church*, Deseret News Press, Salt Lake City, 1960; pp. 178-182; 439-443.
15. *Ibid.* p. 534.
16. *Ibid.* pp. 535-537. See also: *The Instructor*, The Church of Jesus Christ of Latter-day Saints, Salt Lake City, April 1964; inside back cover.

17. Barker, James L., *Apostasy from the Divine Church*, Deseret News Press, Salt Lake City, 1960; pp. 191-193. See also: The Instructor, The Church of Jesus Christ of Latter-day Saints, Salt Lake City, April 1964; inside back cover.

18 Barker, James L., *Apostasy from the Divine Church*, Deseret News Press, Salt Lake City, 1960; pp. 587-588.

19. *Ibid.* pp. 548-549.

20. *Ibid.* pp. 178-181. See also: *The Instructor*, The Church of Jesus Christ of Latter-day Saints, Salt Lake City, April 1964; inside back cover.

21. Barker, James L., *Apostasy from the Divine Church*, Deseret News Press, Salt Lake City, 1960; pp. 41; 410; 619; 650.

22. *Ibid.* p. 653. See also: Talmage, James E., *The Great Apostasy*, Deseret Book, Salt Lake City, 1968; pp. 144-147.

23. Barker, James L., *Apostasy from the Divine Church*, Deseret News Press, Salt Lake City, 1960; p. 247.

24. *Ibid.* pp. 251-254.

25. *Ibid.* p. 325.

26. *Ibid.* pp. 558-565; 641-648.

27. *Ibid.* pp. 560, 598.

28. *Ibid.* p. 633.

29. *Ibid.* p. 656.

30. Petersen, Mark E., *Peter and "The Rock,"* Missionary tract, The Church of Jesus Christ of Latter-day Saints, Salt Lake City; p. 4. See also: Barker, James L., *Apostasy from the Divine Church,* Deseret News Press, Salt Lake City, 1960; pp. 627-629.

31. *Ibid.* p. 4.

32. *Ibid.* p. 6.

33. Barker, James L., *Apostasy from the Divine Church*, Deseret News Press, Salt Lake City, 1960; pp. 574-580.

34. *Ibid.* pp. 558-565, 641-648.

35. *Ibid.* p. 596.

36 *Ibid.* p 638

37. Talmage, James E., *The Great Apostasy*, Deseret Book, Salt Lake City, 1968; p. 143. See also: Barker, James L., *Apostasy from the Divine Church,* Deseret News Press, Salt Lake City, 1960; p. 600.

38. Talmage, James E., *The Great Apostasy,* Deseret Book, Salt Lake City, 1968; p.147.

39. *Ibid.* pp. 144-147. See also: Barker, James L., *Apostasy from the Divine Church*, Deseret News Press, Salt Lake City, 1960; p. 653.

40. *Ibid.* pp 588-590.

41. *Ibid.* p. 689.
42. Petersen, Mark E., *The Great Prologue,* Deseret Book, Salt Lake City, 1975; pp. 28, 29. See also: *Church News,* The Church of Jesus Christ of Latter-day Saints, Salt Lake City, October 1992.
43. "The Falling Away and Restoration of the Gospel of Jesus Christ Foretold," Missionary Department brochure, The Church of Jesus Christ of Latter-day Saints, Salt Lake City.
44. *Ibid.*
45. *Ibid.*
46. Petersen, Mark E., *The Great Prologue,* Deseret Book, Salt Lake City, 1975; pp. 32-48.
47. *Ibid.* pp. 68-89.
48. *Ibid.* p. 103.

5
Joseph Smith

In 1820, a young man named Joseph Smith wanted to know which church he should join. He read in the Bible: "If any of you lack wisdom, let him ask of God and it shall be given him" (James 1:5). Joseph went into a grove of trees near his father's farm in upstate New York and knelt to pray. He later wrote:

> *I saw a pillar of light exactly over my head, above the brightness of the sun, which descended gradually until it fell upon me. When the light rested upon me, I saw two Personages whose brightness and glory defy all description, standing above me in the air. One of them spake unto me, calling me by name and said, pointing to the other, "This is My Beloved Son. Hear Him!" (Joseph Smith History 1:16, 17).*

Joseph was told not to join any church and he later learned that he would be the Lord's instrument in restoring the ancient Church of Jesus Christ to the earth. As members of The Church of Jesus Christ of Latter-day Saints, we do not worship Joseph Smith. We worship Heavenly Father in the name of his Son, Jesus Christ. We revere Joseph Smith as a prophet, like Moses, or Noah, or Abraham. As we learn about the life and accomplishments of Joseph Smith, it becomes easier to accept Joseph as a prophet called of God.

The following are some of the accomplishments of Joseph Smith:

Joseph was a prophet, seer and revelator. As a prophet, he made more than 1,500 prophecies and promises that have been fulfilled or are in the process of being fulfilled.[1] Let me present just five examples.

1) He prophesied many of the specific events of the Civil War, thirty years before they happened. They included the fact that the war would start in South Carolina, that the South would call on Great Britain for help, and that the war would bring death and misery to many souls.[2]

2) He prophesied that the Lamanites (Native Americans) would blossom as a rose, referring to the fact that many would

choose to become members of the Church.[3] The Church currently baptizes a sufficient number of converts to populate approximately two stakes per week in Latin America.[4]

3)   Joseph Smith told Stephen A. Douglas that if he (Douglas) ever turned his back on the Latter-day Saints, he would feel the weight of the Almighty upon him. In 1857, Mr. Douglas spoke against the Saints and, surprisingly, he later suffered a humiliating defeat in which Abraham Lincoln became President of the United States.[5]

4)   The night before Joseph was murdered he told Dan Jones in the Carthage Jail that he (Jones) would "yet see Wales" and accomplish his life's mission. Dan later went to Wales and helped convert more than 15,000 persons to the Church.[6]

5)   As a seventeen-year-old, living in an obscure village, Joseph stated an angel told him his name would be known among all the nations in the world.[7] As of fifty years ago, there were over 20,000 pamphlets or books that discuss Joseph Smith as compared to fewer than 3,000 that discuss George Washington.[8] A count today would reveal thousands more pamphlets and books about Joseph Smith.

As prophet, seer and revelator, Joseph revealed the lost doctrines of the original Church of Jesus Christ. We can read about most of these doctrines in the Bible but, to my knowledge, not one of the other thousands of Christian churches in the world believes even one of them. For example, there should be apostles and prophets in the true church until all come to "the unity of the faith" (Ephesians 4:11-13; 2:20). No other church has apostles and prophets today.

The Bible mentions the Melchizedek and Levitical Priesthoods (Hebrews 6:20; 7:11). No other church professes either priesthood authority. High priests and seventies are mentioned in Hebrews 5:10 and Luke 10:1. No other church I know of has high priests or seventies. There are three kingdoms of God including the Celestial and Terrestrial (1 Corinthians 15:40); 2 Corinthians 12:2 also discusses a third heaven. No other church has this doctrine today.

Before this earthly life began, there was a pre-mortal existence (Jeremiah 1:5). No other church accepts this doctrine today. The Bible also mentions a paradise (Luke 23:43). No other church today teaches of a place called paradise that is different from heaven. A spirit prison is discussed in 1 Peter 3:19 and 4:6. No other church teaches of a spirit prison.

Baptism for the dead is mentioned in 1 Corinthians 15:29. No other church has this doctrine. Amos 3:7 mentions the importance of prophets and revelation. No other church believes in modern-day revelation. Acts 8:17 speaks of the laying on of hands for the Gift of the Holy Ghost. I know of no other church today with this doctrine.

Christ has a body of flesh and bones (Luke 24:39) and Christ will return to the earth in this same form (Acts 1:11). Man is created in the image of God (Genesis 1:27). No other church today believes that God has a body. Matthew 3:16, 17 clearly states that Heavenly Father, Jesus Christ, and the Holy Ghost are separate and distinct personages. No other church believes this.

The Savior gave Peter the keys of sealing or marriage in heaven (Matthew 16:19). No other church believes in this beautiful doctrine. The members of the Church were called saints (Romans 1:7; Philippians 1:1). No other church does this today. Ezekiel 37:16-19 speaks of the coming forth of another book, which is the record of Joseph of Israel, and John 10:16 says Christ will teach "other sheep." No other church has an answer for these scriptures.

Romans 8:16, 17 says we are the spirit children of Heavenly Father and that we can become gods, even joint-heirs with Christ; Psalms 82:6 also says we can become gods. Other churches say this is blasphemy.

Along with revealing the biblical doctrines noted above, Joseph Smith, as a seer and revelator, gave us new or expanded knowledge about a full spectrum of gospel topics.[9] These include the nature of the Godhead; the role and functions of the Holy Ghost; the nature of intelligences; the pre-mortal existence; the Council in Heaven; Jesus Christ's and Lucifer's pre-mortal roles; the Creation, the Fall and the Atonement.

Joseph also spoke of family and parental responsibilities; priesthood keys, organization and ordinances; laws of consecration and stewardship; temple endowments and sealings; work for the dead; spirit paradise and spirit prison; the Second Coming of Jesus Christ; the three degrees of glory and outer darkness.

Joseph translated The Book of Mormon. He did this in only sixty-three days at the early age of only twenty-three.[10] He had only three years of schooling.[11] Emma Smith, his wife, stated that at the time he translated The Book of Mormon, he was not even capable of writing or dictating a well worded letter.[12]

After translating the book, Joseph never went back to review even a single passage. In the morning, when he began translating each day, he never asked his scribe to review where he had left off the day before.[13] The book was published without ever having been reviewed, even once, yet it has remained virtually unchanged for more than 170 years. Can you imagine writing a research paper or a book and never reviewing it before declaring it complete?

Joseph translated an average of nine pages per day. Expert translators average one page per day.[14] The King James Version of the Bible was produced by fifty English scholars over a seven-year period of time. They averaged much less than one page per day![14]

Joseph was President of the Church. As president, Joseph Smith was visited by and received priesthood keys from over fifty heavenly messengers. These messengers included even Heavenly Father, who visited Joseph at least five times.[15] Jesus Christ visited Joseph at least seven times.[16] Moroni led Joseph to the gold plates, which were translated into The Book of Mormon. He visited Joseph at least 22 times.[17]

John the Baptist visited Joseph and brought him the Aaronic Priesthood.[18] Peter, James and John restored the Melchizedek Priesthood.[19] Moses brought the keys of the Gathering of Israel.[20] Elijah brought the keys of sealing individual and families.[21] Elias brought the gospel of Abraham.[22] The angel Gabriel (who is also known as Noah) brought the keys of the restoration of the earth.[23] Raphael (who was either Enoch or a prophet at the time of Enoch) brought the keys of translation as the City of Enoch was translated or lifted up into heaven.[24] Michael, who was Adam, brought Joseph keys as the presiding high priest over the earth.[25] Joseph was also visited by Nephi,[26] Alma,[27] Mormon,[28] Enos,[29] Abel,[30] Methuselah,[31] Paul,[32] Eve,[33] Seth,[34] Abraham,[35] Isaac,[36] Jacob,[37] Joseph,[38] Enoch,[39] the Jewish apostles,[40] and the Nephite disciples.[41]

Joseph was an author of books. Joseph wrote twelve books in addition to translating The Book of Mormon. They include *The Doctrine and Covenants, The Pearl of Great Price, the Inspired Version of the Bible* wherein he made hundreds of corrections, and the *Lectures on Faith.* Many of his writings and talks are compiled in the *Teachings of the Prophet Joseph Smith,* and he wrote seven volumes of *The History of the Church,* each of which is a comprehensive historical work. Joseph added 900 new pages of scripture.[42] All this he did having only three years of formal education.

In addition to English, Joseph learned Reformed Egyptian, Hebrew, Greek, and German.[43] He said that if he lived long enough, he would learn every language on the face of the earth.[44] He formed the School of the Prophets, which was the first form of adult education in America.[45]

Joseph was a designer and builder of temples. He revealed God's purpose for temples.[46] He revealed the specific ordinances of the temple, word for word,[47] as well as the temple clothes and temple garments. Numerous articles have been written recently about similar garments, markings and sacred clothing found among ancient peoples.[48] Mummies have been discovered recently with similar garments and markings.[49]

Joseph started what has become the largest genealogical program in the world.[50] He designed and built the Kirtland Temple, and he also designed and built the Nauvoo Temple in 1844 at a cost of over $1 million.[51] He commenced the great ordinance work for the dead. Only after all these things were revealed for the exaltation of man, would the Lord permit his life to be taken.

Joseph was a founder and mayor of cities and communities. He formed cities in New York, Ohio, Missouri, and Illinois. He pointed the way for the gathering of the Saints in the Rocky Mountains. He designed and planned the City of Zion, which is yet to be built.[52] Joseph planned, organized, and built the City of Nauvoo, which was the largest city in Illinois at that time.[53]

Salt Lake City is patterned after the City of Zion and the City of Nauvoo in terms of the size of city blocks, the width of streets, the numbering of city blocks and the city design, which is centered around the temple.

Joseph implemented the United Order, the law of tithing and the basics of the Church welfare program, which is unparalleled in the world today.[54] Leaders of nations have come from around the world to examine the welfare program of the Church.

Joseph was a lieutenant general. He directed a militia that was second only in size to the United States Army at that time.[55, 56] To receive this honor he was chosen by a vote of the people and commissioned by the Governor of Illinois. He led Zion's Camp, a military march from Ohio to Missouri. The organization he implemented was used for the exodus from Illinois to Utah some years later.

At the time of his death *Joseph was a candidate for president of the United States.* As a candidate, he frequently spoke about women's rights, prison reform, a national banking system, territorial expansion, and the liberation of slaves.[57] Some of these topics are still important issues today.

Joseph was a good husband and a good father to his children. During their seventeen years of marriage, Joseph and Emma were parents to eleven children, two of whom were adopted. Six of the eleven children died in infancy or childhood. Alvin lived just a few moments. Thaddeus and Louisa, who were twins, lived three hours. Don Carlos lived fourteen months, and an unnamed infant boy died at birth. Joseph Murdock lived only eleven months.

Joseph was tried in court approximately sixty times on false charges.[58]Following one of these he was imprisoned in Liberty Jail for four months. During this time he wrote frequent and loving letters to his family and tender entries in his journal.[59, 60]

To review, Joseph was a prophet, seer, and revelator. He translated The Book of Mormon. He was President of The Church of Jesus Christ of Latter-day Saints, was author of many books, translator of languages, designer and builder of temples, founder and mayor of cities and communities, lieutenant general in the state militia, candidate for president of the United States, and a good husband and father.

Joseph Smith changed the world. Any of these listed items would qualify as important, lifetime accomplishments. Yet, Joseph was martyred when he was only thirty-eight years old. He did all of these things during a span of only fifteen years. When he died Emma was four months pregnant and their other children were six, eight, eleven, and thirteen. Joseph and his brother Hyrum were murdered together, sealing their testimonies with their blood. Their mother wrote about that terrible day:

> After the corpses were washed and dressed in their burial clothes, we were allowed to see them . . . When I entered the room, it was too much; I sank back, crying to the Lord in the agony of my soul, "My God, my God, why hast thou forsaken this family!" A voice replied, "I have taken them to myself, that they might have rest." Emma was carried back to her room almost in a state of insensibility. Her oldest son

approached the corpse and dropped upon his knees, and laying his cheek against his father's and kissing him, exclaimed, "Oh, my father! my father!"

As I looked upon their peaceful, smiling countenances, I seemed almost to hear them say, "Mother, weep not for us; we have overcome the world by love; we have carried to them the gospel that their souls might be saved; they slew us for our testimony, and thus placed us beyond their power; their ascendancy is for a moment; ours is an eternal triumph."[61]

As a testimony to the world, Joseph wrote:

I saw a pillar of light exactly over my head, above the brightness of the sun, which descended gradually until it fell upon me. When the light rested upon me, I saw two personages whose brightness and glory defy all description, standing above me in the air. One of them spake unto me, calling me by name and said, pointing to the other, "This is My Beloved Son. Hear Him!" I had seen a vision; I knew it, and I knew that God knew it.[62]

I want you to know that I also know it.

Notes:

1. Madsen, Truman G., *Joseph Smith the Prophet,* Bookcraft, Salt Lake City, Utah, 1990; p. 37. (Reports that Elder John A. Widtsoe said The Doctrine and Covenants contains 1,100 statements of the future; along with many other statements, Joseph's prophecies exceed 1,500.)
2. Doctrine and Covenants 87.
3. Doctrine and Covenants 49:24.
4. *Ensign*, The Church of Jesus Christ of Latter-day Saints, Salt Lake City, August 1993, p. 75. (Reports that in 1992 there were 1.5 million members in South America. *Ensign*, February 1997, p. 75 says in mid-1996, the members in South America reached 2.0 million.) This growth, plus the growth in Central America equates to about two new stakes per week.
5. Benson, Ezra Taft, "Joseph Smith, Prophet in Our Generation," *Ensign*, The Church of Jesus Christ of Latter-day Saints, Salt Lake City, March 1994; p. 4.
6. Madsen, Truman G., *Joseph Smith the Prophet,* Bookcraft, Salt Lake City, Utah, 1990; p. 40.

7. *Joseph Smith History* 1:33, The Pearl of Great Price, The Church of Jesus Christ of Latter-day Saints, Salt Lake City, 1981.
8. Evans, John Henry, *Joseph Smith: An American Prophet,* The MacMillan Co., New York, 1946; pp. 319, 320. (Reports that the Church Historian's Office has over 20,000 volumes, each of which talk of Joseph Smith and there are only 2,556 volumes in the Library of Congress that speak of George Washington.) Also see Haroldsen, Edwin O., "Good and Evil Spoken Of," *Ensign,* The Church of Jesus Christ of Latter-day Saints, Salt Lake City; August 1995; pp. 8-11.
9. Lund, Gerald N., "A Prophet for the Fulness of Times," *Ensign,* The Church of Jesus Christ of Latter-day Saints, Salt Lake City, January 1997; pp. 52, 53.
10. Welch, J. W. and Tim Rathbone, *The Translation of The Book of Mormon: Preliminary Report on the Basic Historical Information,* FARMS, Provo, Utah, 1986; pp. 38, 39.
11. Backman, Milton V. Jr., "Lo, Here! Lo, There! Early in the Spring of 1820," *The Prophet Joseph, Essays on the Life and Mission of Joseph Smith,* Porter, Larry C. and Susan Easton Black, Eds., Deseret Book, Salt Lake City, 1988; p. 19.
12. Joseph Smith III, Ed., "Last Testimony of Sister Emma," *Saints Advocate,* 4, Reorganized Church of Jesus Christ of Latter-day Saints, Independence, Mo., October 1879; pp. 49-52.
13. Skousen, Royal, "Translating The Book of Mormon," *The Book of Mormon Authorship Revisited,* Reynolds, Noel B., Ed., FARMS, Provo, Utah 1997; pp. 62, 63.
14. Nelson, Russell M., "A Testimony of The Book of Mormon," Ensign, The Church of Jesus Christ of Latter-day Saints, Salt Lake City, November 1999; p. 71. See also Maxwell, Neal A., "My Servant Joseph," *Ensign,* The Church of Jesus Christ of Latter-day Saints, Salt Lake City, May 1992; p. 38.
15. Father's visits: a. The First Vision, *Joseph Smith History* 1:17, *The Pearl of Great Price,* The Church of Jesus Christ of Latter-day Saints, Salt Lake City, 1981; b. At the Isaac Morley farm, June 1831, Joseph said: "I Now See God, and Jesus Christ at his right hand." Lyman Wight also saw them. (Perkins, Keith W., "The Prophet Joseph Smith in 'The Ohio': The Schoolmaster," *The Prophet Joseph, Essays on the Life and Mission of Joseph Smith,* Porter, Larry C. and Susan Easton Black, Eds., Deseret Book, Salt Lake City, 1988; p. 96.) c. D&C 76:20-23 d. Zebedee Coltrin said, "I saw a person passing through the room as plainly as I see you

now. Joseph asked us if we knew who it was and answered himself, 'That is Jesus our Elder Brother, the Son of God.' Again I saw passing through the same room, a personage whose glory and brightness was so great, that I can liken it to nothing but the burning bush that Moses saw, and its power was so great that had it continued much longer I believe it would have consumed us. The Prophet Joseph said this was the Father of the Lord Jesus Christ. I saw him." John Murdock saw them at the same time (*Ibid.* pp. 110, 111. See also: Backman, Milton V., Jr. and Cowan, Richard O., "Joseph Smith and the Doctrine and Covenants," Deseret Book, Salt Lake City, 1992; p. 78 and *Ensign,* The Church of Jesus Christ of Latter-day Saints, Salt Lake City, January 1993; p. 37.) e. The First Presidency saw the Father and the Son and received D&C 137. (See Perkins, Keith W., "The Prophet Joseph Smith in 'The Ohio': The Schoolmaster," *The Prophet Joseph, Essays on the Life and Mission of Joseph Smith,* Porter, Larry C. and Susan Easton Black, Eds., Deseret Book, Salt Lake City, 1988; p. 100.)

16. Jesus Christ's visits: (See note 15 for visits a through e.) f. Prophet's parents' home; 1831, Joseph and Martin Harris saw Christ.(Perkins, Keith W., "The Prophet Joseph Smith in 'The Ohio': The Schoolmaster," *The Prophet Joseph, Essays on the Life and Mission of Joseph Smith,* Porter, Larry C. and Susan Easton Black, Eds., Deseret Book, Salt Lake City, 1988; p. 96). See also Don L. Searle, "A Disciple in Deed," *Ensign,* The Church of Jesus Christ of Latter-day Saints, Salt Lake City, June 1994, p. 15.) g. D&C 110:2, 3.

17. Peterson, H. Donl, "Moroni: Joseph Smith's Tutor," *Ensign,* The Church of Jesus Christ of Latter-day Saints, Salt Lake City, January 1992, pp. 28, 29.

18. D&C 13:1.

19. D&C 27:12.

20. D&C 110:11.

21. D&C 110:13.

22. D&C 110:12.

23. D&C 128:21; McConkie, Bruce R., *The Millennial Messiah,* Deseret Book, Salt Lake City, Utah, 1982; pp. 119, 120.

24. D&C 128:21; McConkie, Bruce R., *The Millennial Messiah,* Deseret Book, Salt Lake City, Utah, 1982; pp. 119, 120.

25. D&C 128:21; McConkie, Bruce R., *The Millennial Messiah,* Deseret Book, Salt Lake City, Utah, 1982; pp. 119, 120.

26. *Journal of Discourses,* Latter-day Saint's Book Depot, London, England, 1886; 13:47.
27. *Ibid.* 13:47.
28. *Ibid.* 17:374.
29. *Ibid.* 18:325.
30. *Ibid.* 18:325.
31. *Ibid.* 18:325.
32. Smith, Joseph Fielding, Compiler, *Teachings of the Prophet Joseph Smith,* Deseret Book, Salt Lake City, Utah, 1982; p. 180.
33. Huntington Oliver B., *Diary,* part 2, Brigham Young University Library, Provo, Utah; p. 244.
34. *Journal of Discourses,* Latter-day Saints Book Depot, London, England, 1886; 21:94.
35. D&C 27:10.
36. D&C 27:10; *Journal of Discourses,* Latter-day Saints Book Depot, London, England, 1886; 21:94.
37. D&C 27:10; *Journal of Discourses,* Latter-day Saints Book Depot, London, England, 1886; 21:94.
38. D&C 27:10.
39. *Journal of Discourses,* Latter-day Saints Book Depot, London, England, 1886; 21:65.
40. *Journal of Discourses,* Latter-day Saints Book Depot, London, England, 1886; 21:94.
41. *Journal of Discourses,* Latter-day Saints Book Depot, London, England, 1886; 21:94. See also Smith, Brian L., "I Have a Question," *Ensign,* The Church of Jesus Christ of Latter-day Saints, Salt Lake City, October 1994; pp. 63, 64. See also: Millet, Robert L., "Joseph Smith Among the Prophets," *Ensign,* The Church of Jesus Christ of Latter-day Saints, Salt Lake City, June 1994; p. 20.
42. Lund, Gerald N., "A Prophet for the Fulness of Times," *Ensign,* The Church of Jesus Christ of Latter-day Saints, Salt Lake City, January 1997; pp. 50-54.
43. Berrett, Dr. William E., *BYU Speeches of the Year,* "The Life and Character of the Prophet Joseph Smith," April 21, 1964, Brigham Young University, Provo, Utah, 1964; p. 4.
44. *Ibid.* p. 4.
45. Matthews, Robert J., "Contributions of the Prophet Joseph Smith," *The Instructor,* The Church of Jesus Christ of Latter-day Saints, Salt Lake City, November 1965; inside back cover.
46. *Ibid.,* inside back cover.

47. Woodruff, Wilford, General Conference, April 1894, as quoted by Packer, Boyd K., *The Holy Temple,* Bookcraft, Salt Lake City, 1980; p. 199.

48. Nibley, Hugh, *Mormonism and Early Christianity*, FARMS, Provo, Utah, 1987; pp. 61, 62. See also: Nibley, Hugh, *Temples and Cosmos,* FARMS, Provo, Utah, 1992; pp. 91-173.

49. Griggs, C. Wilfred, Know Your Religion Speeches, author's notes, 1995. See also: Nibley, Hugh, *Temples and Cosmos,* FARMS, Provo, Utah, 1992; pp. 107-111.

50. D&C 127, 117, 128.

51. *Teachings of Presidents of the Church: Joseph F. Smith,* The Church of Jesus Christ of Latter-day Saints, Salt Lake City, 1998; p. 18.

52. Arrington, Leonard J., "Joseph Smith, Builder of Ideal Communities," *The Prophet Joseph, Essays on the Life and Mission of Joseph Smith,* Porter, Larry C. and Susan Easton Black, Eds., Deseret Book, Salt Lake City, 1988; pp. 115-137.

53. Cannon, David Q., "The Founding of Nauvoo," *The Prophet Joseph, Essays on the Life and Mission of Joseph Smith,* Porter, Larry C. and Susan Easton Black, Eds., Deseret Book, Salt Lake City, 1988; pp. 250+.

54. Nibley, Preston, *The Presidents of the Church,* Deseret Book, Salt Lake City, 1971; p. 24. See also: Madsen, Truman G., *Joseph Smith the Prophet,* Bookcraft, Salt Lake City, Utah, 1990; pp. 61, 109.

55. Matthews, Robert J., "Contributions of the Prophet Joseph Smith," *The Instructor,* The Church of Jesus Christ of Latter-day Saints, Salt Lake City, November 1965; inside back cover. Madsen, Truman G., *Joseph Smith the Prophet,* Bookcraft, Salt Lake City, Utah, 1990; p. 109. See also: Joseph Fielding Smith, Church History and Modern Revelation, Vol. 4, The Council of the Twelve Apostles of The Church of Jesus Christ of Latter-day Saints, Salt Lake City, 1946; p. 65.

56. Madsen, Truman G., *Joseph Smith the Prophet,* Bookcraft, Salt Lake City, Utah, 1990; p. 101.

57. Matthews, Robert J., "Contributions of the Prophet Joseph Smith," *The Instructor,* The Church of Jesus Christ of Latter-day Saints, Salt Lake City, November 1965; inside back cover.

58. Ludlow, Daniel H., Ed., *Encyclopedia of Mormonism,* Vol. 3, MacMillan Publishing Company, New York, 1992; p. 1346. Bentley, Joseph I., *Joseph Smith: Legal Trials,* NY, MacMillan, 1992.

(Reports that Joseph faced thirty criminal actions and at least that many civil suits.)

59. Backman, Milton V., Jr. and Richard O. Cowan, *Joseph Smith and the Doctrine and Covenants,* Deseret Book Co., Salt Lake City, 1992, pp. 126, 127. See also: Ludlow, Daniel H., Ed., *Encyclopedia of Mormonism,* Vol. 3, MacMillan Publishing Company, New York, 1992; p. 1346

60. Jones, Gracia N., "Emma Hale Smith," *Ensign,* The Church of Jesus Christ of Latter-day Saints, Salt Lake City, August 1992; p. 34.

61. Smith, Lucy Mack, *History of Joseph Smith,* Bookcraft, Salt Lake City, pp. 324, 325.

62. *Joseph Smith History,* Deseret Book, Salt Lake City, 1980; 1:16, 17, 25.

6
The Book of Mormon

As part of the restoration of the Church of Jesus Christ, Joseph Smith was led by the angel Moroni to gold plates that were buried in a hill near Joseph's home. Through divine help Joseph translated the plates and published The Book of Mormon, which includes the writings of prophets of ancient civilizations on the American continent between 2200 B.C. and 421 A.D. It also includes the account of the visit of Jesus Christ to America after his resurrection.

The Book of Mormon is a key to receiving a testimony or witness of the truthfulness of The Church of Jesus Christ of Latter-day Saints. It is a witness of the divinity of Jesus Christ. If The Book of Mormon is true then Joseph Smith was surely a prophet called of God, and The Church of Jesus Christ of Latter-day Saints is true.

In this chapter I would like to present information about the truthfulness of The Book of Mormon, somewhat as if it were on trial in a court of law. I would first call **Emma Smith,** the wife of Joseph. She would testify that The Book of Mormon was translated in only sixty-three days by her twenty-three-year-old husband who had only three years of formal education.[1, 2] Emma once said that during the time he was translating the book Joseph was not even capable of dictating or writing a well worded letter to a friend.[3] It is interesting to note that an experienced translator can normally translate about one page per day.[4] Joseph averaged nine pages a day.

If **Oliver Cowdery** were called to testify, he would say he served as scribe and that Joseph vocally dictated the words from the gold plates to him. Joseph never went back to review the translated passages. As he began translation he never asked Oliver to review for him where he left off the previous day.[5] Furthermore, Oliver would state that The Book of Mormon was published without ever having been reviewed. Except for corrections such as punctuation it has remained virtually unchanged for more than 170 years.

I would next call on some **"wordprint" experts** to testify about computer generated analyses that have been completed on the book. These extensive analyses have been conducted comparing the syntax, sentence structure, and vocabulary used by the authors of the various parts or books of The Book of Mormon.[6] They have compared these analyses with the original writings of Joseph Smith, some of his associates, and others who some have thought might have written the book. These experts have included both members and nonmembers of the Church.

All of these analyses show that The Book of Mormon was in fact written by several *different* authors, just as it claims. In addition, the studies all prove that the word usage and other indicators of authorship clearly demonstrate the book was *not* written by Joseph Smith nor by *any* of his known contemporaries. These statistical experts also state that it would be impossible to fake the word patterns or wordprints of the different authors.

I would next call a **Hebrew scholar** who would testify that in the past thirty years researchers have found that The Book of Mormon contains many examples of Chiasmus, which is a unique form of Hebrew writing.[7] Chiasmus, which was discovered only about fifty years ago, exists throughout ancient Hebrew writings such as the Bible. An example of Chiasmus is found in Psalms 3:7, 8 (literally translated from the Hebrew language).

1. Save me,
   2. O my God,
      3.for thou has smitten
         4. all my enemies
            5. on the cheekbone;
            5. The teeth
         4. of the wicked
      3. thou hast broken;
   2. to Jehovah,
1. the salvation.

As one can see, the 1s match, as do the 2s, 3s, 4s, and 5s. Using computers, scholars have found very complex forms of Chiasmus in The Book of Mormon, extending over many verses.[8] Chiasmus has also been found in other ancient Mayan literature.[9] It was not even recognized in the modern world prior to the twentieth century.[10] This fact alone appears to prove The Book of Mormon is of Hebraic origin.

The Hebrew scholar would also testify that there are many other forms of Hebraic writing in the text of The Book of Mormon.

Recently several volumes have been written on this subject.[11] Some examples of the forms of Hebraic writing, which appear awkward when translated literally into English, include such examples of the *construct state* as: "plates of brass, "works of righteousness," "words of plainness," "night of darkness," and "rod of iron." Examples of *adverbials* include: "with patience," "with joy," and "with gladness." Examples of *cognates* include "work all manner of work," "judge righteous judgments," "taxed with a tax," and "cursed with a cursing." Examples of *conjunctions* include: "and he left his house, and the land of his inheritance, and his gold, and his silver, and his precious things, and took nothing with him, save it were his family and provisions and tents and he departed."

Examples of *naming* conventions include: "called the name of the city Moroni," "called their names Mosiah, and Helorum and Helaman." Examples of *possessive pronouns* include: "the words of me," "eyes of me," "power of him."

Many Native American religious customs are identical to customs of the Hebrews and many of their words closely resemble Hebrew words.[12] Examples include the following:

English	Indian	Hebrew
Heavens	Hemin	Hemim
Man	Ishte	Ish
Woman	Ishto	Ishto
Winter	Kora	Korah
Pray	Phale	Phalac
Man of God	Ishto Alle	Ishda Alloah
God	Ale	Ale, Aleim
Father	Abba	Abba
Name	Na	Na

Several books have been written about Hebrew symbols in ancient Native American rock drawings dating back to pre-Columbian periods.[13] A stone found in Bat Creek, Tennessee has been traced to pre-Columbian times and actually contains Hebrew symbols.[14] When older generations of Maoris in New Zealand chant their genealogy the chant ends with a man named Hagoth, which is the name of the man in the book of Alma in The Book of Mormon who sailed away with many people.[15]

There was a general in Israel around 600 B.C. who came from a place called Lachish. He was sent by the king to find some families who left Jerusalem and went toward Egypt taking with them some ancient records. The general wrote several letters to the king called the "Lachish letters," in which he stated that he was unable to find the families or the records. There are many other parallels between the content of these letters and the story of Lehi and his family in The Book of Mormon.[16]

The Book of Mormon states that King Zedekiah's son Mulek left the Middle East and went to the New World. Since the time when The Book of Mormon was published, scholars have stated that King Zedekiah's sons were all executed in Babylon. But more recently, some scholars of the ancient Middle East have reported that Zedekiah may have had a son named Mulek who escaped execution.[17]

In the desert south of Jerusalem, an ancient cave has been discovered that contains drawings of two ships. The drawings have been dated to the sixth century B.C. and some archeologists have come to believe that the inscriptions were the work of a prophet who was fleeing Jerusalem. Khirbet Beit Lei, the name of the cave, means "Ruin of the House of Lehi."[18] Part of the cave is displayed in the Hebrew University Museum.

In The Book of Mormon where Zemnarihah's execution is reported (3 Nephi 4:28), the tree from which he was hanged was ritually chopped down. Recently it was discovered that this bizarre ritual was part of ancient Jewish law, which required that the tree from which a person was hanged must be chopped down.[19]

Recent research on King Benjamin's marvelous speech in Mosiah, chapters two through five, shows that the sermon is linked with the ancient Israelite Feast of Tabernacles and the Day of Atonement as well as early Near Eastern coronation festivals.[20] Joseph Smith could not have learned this from the Bible nor from other books that were available to him.

The next witness I would call would be an *Egyptologist*. Many of the 180 names of people and places used in The Book of Mormon, which are not found elsewhere in the English language, such as Moroni, Ammon, Nephi, Manti and Lehi are actually ancient Egyptian or Hebrew names.[21] Names such as Sariah[22] and Alma,[23] are not known as Hebrew names, but have since been found in ancient Jewish documents found in Egypt. The letters q, x, and w are not found in proper names in The Book of Mormon. Neither are these letters found in ancient Hebrew proper names.[24]

Scholars have also concluded that many Book of Mormon suffixes and prefixes, as well as writing style, sentence structure, and phraseology match ancient Egyptian and Hebrew languages.[25] Even Nephi's opening statement: "I Nephi, having been born of goodly parents . . ." is modeled after the writing style of ancient Egyptians.[26] Research of these cultures was not conducted until more than 100 years after The Book of Mormon was published.

The Egyptologist would also testify that the pyramids discovered in Central America are similar to the pyramids in Egypt both inside and out. Pyramids found in the ancient American city of Copán and San Juan Teotihuacán, México are close in size to the Great Pyramid of Giza in Egypt.[27] A pyramid in Cholula, México is the world's largest known pyramid and is twice the base measurement of the Great Pyramid of Egypt.[28]

This witness would testify that recent discoveries indicate that from 900 B.C. to 600 B.C., several texts in Hebrew and Aramaic (the languages used by the Jews in Lehi's time) were written in Egyptian characters. While the script was Egyptian, the underlying language was Hebrew or Aramaic. Lehi and his progenitors did this because it took less space for Egyptian characters than Hebrew or Aramaic.[29]

I would call an **historian** next who would testify that the book contains 239 chapters: fifty-four about wars, twenty-one about history, fifty-five about prophecy, seventy-one about doctrine, seventeen about missionaries and twenty-one about the mission of Jesus Christ.[30] If the authors of The Book of Mormon had been making up their story as they wrote it, they would have required a computer or another sophisticated system to keep all the names, dates, people, places and ages straight in their minds.

Can you imagine trying to write a lengthy book that spans 2,600 years of history—including wars, political turmoil, and complex religious teachings—without contradictions? Even great authors such as Shakespeare had many inconsistencies and errors in their writings, such as the mentioning of the striking of a clock in *Julius Caesar,* three hundred years before striking clocks were invented.[31] There are no such errors in The Book of Mormon.

The ablest of scholars have examined the book for more than a century and a half and not a single claim or fact in the book has been disproved. Some critics have mentioned things like some of the verses of Isaiah in The Book of Mormon are different from those in the Bible. Recent studies have shown that the Isaiah verses in The Book of Mormon, when compared to the ancient texts, are more accurate than the verses in the King James Version of the Bible.[32] Since Joseph Smith did not have access to the ancient texts, this alone is proof to me that The Book of Mormon is true.

Critics said the hours of Christ's crucifixion are different in the Bible than in The Book of Mormon. However, when adjusted for time zones, the hours are precisely correct, as the reader would expect.[33] In the 1800s people did not know about time zones.

The Book of Mormon contains many chapters describing wars, pointing out to our generation that "wars simply do not work." The world's leaders today should learn this lesson. Studies of the wars in the book have shown them to accurately describe ancient American wars as well as the seasons for wars. Wars were fought consistently during the winter months, the dry season, consistent with ancient Mesoamerican conflicts.[34] The other seasons were reserved for the cultivation and harvesting of crops.

Critics thought the allegory of the olive tree in Jacob chapter five was inaccurate in terms of grafting limbs from certain trees in order for the vineyard to thrive. Recent studies have shown the gardening methods for olive trees as discussed in Jacob chapter five are indeed accurate.[35] Critics laughed at Alma 7:10, which predicted that Jesus would "be born of Mary, at Jerusalem which is the land of our forefathers." Everyone knows that Jesus was born in Bethlehem, not Jerusalem. Recent evidence says, however, that Bethlehem was regarded anciently as a town "in the land of Jerusalem."[36]

I would call an ***anthropologist*** to testify that research has shown there were two major groups of people among these ancient inhabitants:[37] The first group arrived after the dispersion of the inhabitants of the earth. We know this to be the time of the Tower of Babel. The Book calls these people Jaredites, who, it is generally believed, later became the Olmecs. The second group, who, it is generally believed, became the Mayas, has recently been traced back to around 600 B.C., the period mentioned in The Book of Mormon when the Nephites and Lamanites arrived in the promised land.[38] Furthermore, the second group was made up of a people of a lighter skin and of a darker skin who were often at war with each other.[39]

Many history books still say the Native Americans descended from groups that came from Mongolia and the Orient, who crossed the Bering Strait. Some likely did. However, in Mongolia and the Orient, type B blood is very common. Type B is almost nonexistent among Native Americans. Incidentally, blood types among Native Americans are in the same proportion as among Arabs and Jews.[40]

Ancient Mayan writings, such as the *Popol Vuh*, contain words and names that have Egyptian roots of both sounds and meanings. A scholar recently stated that the languages spoken by the Olmecs, as well as by the Mayas of Mexico and Central America are closely related to, and probably descended from, ancient Egyptian.[41]

The Book of Mormon states that Jesus Christ visited ancient American people following his crucifixion in Jerusalem. The anthropologist witness would say that many books have been written about Christ's visit to the Americas.[42] He would also say that virtually all the various groups of inhabitants throughout America believe in a white, bearded god who descended out of heaven.[43] This god healed the sick by laying his hands on them. He brought love as well as commandments and laws to be obeyed.[44] Earthquakes and darkness preceded this god's descent to the people, just as stated in The Book of Mormon.[45]

The people in ancient America also believed the white god would return. This is the reason the Aztecs and other groups completely submitted themselves to Cortez and the other white, bearded conquistadors. They thought the god of their ancestors had returned.[46]

Next I would call a ***theologian*** to testify that these ancient people must have had a record similar to the Old Testament.[47] The Book of Mormon calls this record the brass plates of Laban. The theologian would say these people believed in three Gods: The Father, the Son and the Holy Ghost. They believed they were created in the image of God. They believed in a man named Noah who built a boat, filled it with animals, and survived a great flood brought on by God. They believed God left the rainbow as a sign that he will never again destroy the inhabitants of the earth in this manner. They believed in a tower that was built to reach heaven and in the plagues of Moses.

The theologian would also testify regarding the white, bearded god who descended out of heaven, spoken of by the anthropologist. He would say that these people depicted this god as a plumed serpent.[48] The plumes were because the god descended from heaven. He would also say that many believe the god was like a serpent because it was all-powerful. In addition, the plumed serpent combined the sky with the earth and that because the serpent sheds its skin, it represented overcoming death and beginning a new life.

This witness would also say that in early times, the serpent became identified with the crucifixion and atonement of Jesus Christ.[49] The rod carried by Moses had a serpent on its top indicating eternal life. As John said: "Moses lifted up the serpent in the wilderness, even so must the Son of man be lifted up: That whosoever believeth in him should not perish, but have eternal life" (John 3:14, 15). Even today, physicians in the United States military wear an insignia of a snake as a symbol of life.

Then I would call an *archaeologist* to the stand who would testify of archeological findings, which provide evidence of the truthfulness of The Book of Mormon. Such undeniable evidence includes the discovery of cement used for construction, elephants, horses, copper, wheels, and large cities. These references were scoffed at by scholars for decades. However, research has since proven the existence of all of these among ancient American people.

Scholars laughed in 1830 when The Book of Mormon mentioned the use of cement for construction, which at that time, the world did not know how to use. Over the past fifty years, archeologists have found more than 4,000 miles of highway built using cement by ancient American inhabitants. Such highways are as wide as four lanes of our modern highways, are as deep as fifty feet, down to bedrock, and are built out of a higher grade concrete than we currently have.[50] The buildings of this ancient people have also withstood earthquakes better than modern-day buildings.

Archeologists originally laughed at the mention of elephants in The Book of Mormon. Even when they later found skeletons of elephants in the La Brea tar pits in California, they said such elephants lived during a different period in time than man. However, they then found an elephant skeleton with an arrowhead imbedded in one of its joints.[51]

Scholars also laughed at the mention of horses in The Book of Mormon as they believed horses were brought to America by the Spanish explorers. Since then, however, they have found many paintings made more than 2,000 years ago depicting horses.[52]

Scientists and metallurgists laughed at the mention of copper used for making tools since copper is a soft metal. Over 10,000 ancient tools have since been found, which were made from hardened copper.[53] Even today we are not capable of hardening copper as these ancient people did. Archeologists have found that these people even used hardened copper for surgical tools.

Archeologists did not believe these people had wheels as mentioned in The Book of Mormon. They have since found toys with wheels as well as ancient wheels as large as nine feet in diameter.[54] Scientists thought these people consisted of a few, small nomadic tribes and scoffed at the mention of large cities in The Book of Mormon. They have since found ruins of many ancient cities where more than one million people lived. They have also determined that many of these cities were totally destroyed around 33 A.D., the year Christ was crucified as described in The Book of Mormon.[55] Claims that records were written on gold plates and placed in a stone box were laughed at 170 years ago. Today, scholars admit that metal plates and stone boxes were in standard use for ancient records in many areas of the world.[56]

I would call **Native Americans and Polynesians** as witnesses. The Book of Mormon is consistent with ancient legends passed down from generation to generation for hundreds of years from tribes throughout America and Polynesia.[57] Some examples of these include the white, bearded god who descended from heaven and promised he would return once again. They mention a church founded with twelve disciples that practiced baptism by immersion. The legends speak of three gods including the Father, the Son and the Holy Spirit. Recently discovered Mayan texts, dating from 1554, state that the Mayan ancestors came from where the sun rises and they were descendants of Israel.[58]

I would next call the **three witnesses** to The Book of Mormon. These three men; David Whitmer, Oliver Cowdery, and Martin Harris testified in writing that an angel from heaven appeared to them and showed them the ancient plates. They handled them and felt the engravings. The voice of Christ declared to them that the record was true.[59] These three men received nothing of monetary gain for their testimony. Instead they were severely persecuted. To their dying day, not one of them denied their testimony.

Near the end of David Whitmer's life there were rumors that he had denied his testimony of The Book of Mormon. So, he went to twenty-two influential leaders in the state of Missouri where he lived and asked them to sign an affidavit stating that he was an honest, upright person of highest integrity. Then he wrote his testimony of The Book of Mormon stating he had never denied, nor would he ever, having seen an angel and knowing the book was true. His testimony, and the affidavit, were published in the local newspaper, following which he sent the article to the *New York Times* and the *London Times,* where the article was published, both with worldwide circulation.[60] On David Whitmer's deathbed, he reiterated his testimony.[61] His tombstone in Missouri says, "The Record of the Jews and the Record of the Nephites are One."

When the Saints moved west, Oliver Cowdery moved to Ohio where he became a renowned attorney, state assemblyman, and state senator. On one occasion in court the opposing counsel accused Oliver of being a man who testified that he had seen an angel of God and that the angel had shown him the plates from which The Book of Mormon was translated. On record, in court, Oliver responded that whatever his faults and weaknesses, the testimony he had written was true and he firmly believed in the divinity of the Book.[62]

At the time when Oliver lay on his deathbed, eight people reported on the power of his dying testimony, as he reiterated his firm witness of The Book of Mormon with full knowledge that he faced the closing moments of life. Thirty-seven years later, Oliver's wife wrote a letter that stated: "He always without one doubt . . . affirmed the divinity and truth of The Book of Mormon."[63]

Martin Harris spent the last years of his life testifying among the Saints of the Church in Utah about The Book of Mormon. On Martin's deathbed at the age of ninety-two, George Godfrey deliberately waited for a semiconscious moment to suggest that Martin's testimony was possibly based on deception. His response was vigorous. "I know what I know. I have seen what I have seen and I have heard what I have heard. I have seen the gold plates. . . .An angel appeared to me and others."[64]

The *eight witnesses* to The Book of Mormon and others who saw the plates would then be called to the stand. The eight testified in writing that they handled the gold plates and felt the engravings.[65] At least four additional individuals that we know of lifted and felt the plates: Mary Whitmer, who was shown the plates by the angel Moroni;[66] Joseph's mother, Lucy Mack Smith also saw the breastplate and the Urim and Thummim.[67] Joseph's wife, Emma,[68] and

Joseph's brother, William, saw the plates.[69] Each of these twelve individuals received severe persecution for their testimonies but to their dying day not one of them ever denied seeing or handling the plates.[70]

As a silent witness of the truth, I would present the **Holy Bible.** There are no conflicts between the doctrines of Jesus Christ as presented in The Book of Mormon and as found in the Bible. Instead, there are numerous prophecies throughout the Bible that directly relate to the coming forth of The Book of Mormon. Some examples include the prophecy that the seed of Joseph would spread across the ocean to the everlasting hills (Genesis 49:22, 26). That is exactly what Lehi, a descendant of Joseph, did. Another prophecy in the Bible is that the stick, or writings, of Joseph would join with the stick of Judah (Ezekiel 37:16). The stick of Joseph is The Book of Mormon that has joined the Holy Bible, which is the stick, or book, of Judah as a witness of Jesus Christ.

The Old Testament speaks of truth springing out of the earth (Psalms 85:11). It also speaks of a voice coming from the dust, which is a good description of The Book of Mormon's coming out of the ground (Isaiah 29:4). Isaiah also speaks of a scholar who would be unable to read a sealed book (Isaiah 29:11). Martin Harris took a sample of The Book of Mormon translation to Professor Charles Anthon, who actually stated that he was not able to read a book that was sealed.

The New Testament says Christ went to teach "other sheep" that were not of the same fold (John 10:16). Other churches have no explanation for this scripture. In The Book of Mormon, when the Savior visited the people in America, he referred to the scripture in John and said that these people were his "other sheep" (3 Nephi 15:17-21).

The apostle John wrote: "And I saw another angel flying in the midst of heaven having the everlasting gospel to preach unto them that dwell on the earth" (Revelation 14:6, 7). We commonly refer to this angel as Moroni. I own an old Catholic Bible translated in French in the early 1600s that says in its footnote to this scripture that the "everlasting gospel is a book to come forth."

I would present **The Book of Mormon itself** as a witness. Moroni says that if you want proof that the Book is true,

I would exhort you that ye would ask God, the Eternal Father, in the name of Christ, if these things are not true. And if ye shall ask with a sincere heart, with real intent, having faith in Christ, he will manifest the truth of it unto you by the power of the Holy Ghost (Moroni 10:4).

Thousands of *early members* of the Church, including Joseph Smith himself, David W. Patten, Parley P. Pratt, Hyrum Smith, Orson Hyde and many intellectual giants and scholars in the early days, as well as 6,000 saints whose bodies are strewn across the plains in shallow graves, sacrificed their very lives and sealed in blood their testimonies of The Book of Mormon. *Millions of members of the Church today* live their lives for the Church and they would testify with their whole souls that The Book of Mormon is true and that the Holy Ghost has borne witness of its truthfulness to them.

Would a jury declare the book to be true? I believe the answer is: of course it would. I also testify by the Spirit that The Book of Mormon is the word of God.

Notes:

In the 1960s, Jack H. West wrote a series of articles entitled: "The Trial of the Stick of Joseph." They had to do with his experiences in law school in placing The Book of Mormon on trial. These articles were later published in a book, which is referenced in these notes. Although the majority of evidences mentioned here have come to light after Brother West's articles and book, the concept of the trial is his.

1. Welch, J. W. and Tim Rathbone, "The Translation of The Book of Mormon: Preliminary Report on the Basic Historical Information," Provo, Utah, FARMS, 1986; pp. 38-39. See also: "How Long Did it Take Joseph Smith to Translate The Book of Mormon?" *Ensign*, The Church of Jesus Christ of Latter-day Saints, Salt Lake City, January 1988; p. 47.

2. Gorton, H. Clay, *The Legacy of the Brass Plates of Laban*, Horizon Publishers, Bountiful, Utah, 1994; p. 22. See also: Backman, Milton V. Jr., "Lo, Here! Lo, There! Early in the Spring of 1820," *The Prophet Joseph: Essays on the Life and Mission of Joseph*

Smith, Larry C. Porter and Susan Easton Black, Eds., Deseret Book, Salt Lake City, 1988; p. 19.

3. Joseph Smith III, ed., "Last Testimony of Sister Emma," *Saints Advocate 4,* Reorganized Church of Jesus Christ of Latter-day Saints, Independence, Mo., October 1879; pp. 49-52.

4. Nelson, Russell M., "A Testimony of The Book of Mormon," *Ensign,* The Church of Jesus Christ of Latter-day Saints, Salt Lake City, November 1999, p. 71. See also Maxwell, Neal A., "My Servant Joseph," *Ensign,* The Church of Jesus Christ of Latter-day Saints, Salt Lake City, May 1992; p. 38.

5. Skousen, Royal, "Translating The Book of Mormon," *The Book of Mormon Authorship Revisited,* Noel B. Reynolds, Ed., FARMS, Provo, Utah, 1997; pp. 62, 63. See also: Maxwell, Neal A., "By the Gift and Power of God," *Ensign,* The Church of Jesus Christ of Latter-day Saints, Salt Lake City, January 1997; pp. 26-41.

6. Hilton, John L., "On Verifying Wordprint Studies: Book of Mormon Authorship," *The Book of Mormon Authorship Revisited,* Noel B. Reynolds, Ed., FARMS, Provo, Utah 1997; pp. 225-253. See also: Reexploring The Book of Mormon, John W. Welch, Ed., Deseret Book, Salt Lake City, 1992; pp. 221-226.

7. Welch, John W., "What Does Chiasmus in The Book of Mormon Prove?" *The Book of Mormon Authorship Revisited,* Noel B. Reynolds, Ed., FARMS, Provo, Utah 1997; pp. 199-224.

8. *Reexploring The Book of Mormon,* John W. Welch, Ed., Deseret Book, Salt Lake City, 1992; pp. 230-232. See also: Welch, John W., "A Masterpiece: Alma 36," *Rediscovering The Book of Mormon,* John L. Sorenson and Melvin J. Thornes, Ed., Deseret Book, Salt Lake City, 1991; pp. 114-131. See also: Welch, John W. and J. Gregory Welch, *Charting The Book of Mormon,* FARMS, Provo, Utah, 1999; charts 130-133.

9. *Reexploring The Book of Mormon,* John W. Welch, Ed., Deseret Book, Salt Lake City, 1992; p. 233. See also: Christenson, Allen J., "Chiasmus in Mayan Texts," *Ensign,* The Church of Jesus Christ of Latter-day Saints, Salt Lake City, October 1988; pp. 28-31.

10. Welch, John W. "Chiasmus in The Book of Mormon," *The New Era,* The Church of Jesus Christ of Latter-day Saints, Salt Lake City, Feb. 1972; pp. 6-11.

11. Pinnock, Hugh W., *Finding Biblical Hebrew and Other Ancient Literary Forms in The Book of Mormon,* FARMS, Provo, Utah, 1999. See also: Tvedtnes, John A., "The Hebrew Background of The Book of Mormon," *Rediscovering The Book of Mormon,* John

L. Sorenson and Melvin J. Thornes, Ed., Deseret Book, Salt Lake City, 1991; pp. 77-91. See also: Barney, Kevin L., "Poetic Diction and Parallel Word Pairs in The Book of Mormon," *Journal of Book of Mormon Studies*, FARMS, Provo, 4/2 1995; pp. 15-81.

12. Widtsoe John A. and Franklin S. Harris, Jr., *Seven Claims of The Book of Mormon*, Deseret News Press, Salt Lake City, 1937; p. 103-115. See also: Roberts, B. H., *New Witnesses for God*, Vol. 3, Deseret Book, Salt Lake City, 1951; pp. 46-48. See also: Rich, Ben E., *The Book of Mormon, Scrapbook of Mormon Literature*, Vol. 2, Henry C. Etten & Co., Chicago, 1913; pp. 272-274.

13. Harris, James Roy, Sr., *Southwestern American Indian Rock Art and The Book of Mormon*, Orem, Utah, 1991. See also: Wirth, Diane E., *A Challenge to the Critics*, Horizon Publishers, Bountiful, Utah, 1986; pp. 76-89.

14. Wirth, Diane E., *A Challenge to the Critics*, Horizon Publishers, Bountiful, Utah, 1986; pp. 79, 80.2.

15. As told by a personal friend of the author, who was a missionary in New Zealand. Also see: Loveland, Jerry K., Brigham Young University Studies, Vol. 17, No. 1, pp. 59, 60 which mentions that Thor Heyerdahl had been the leading scholarly exponent of the theory that there were significant migrations of peoples from the Western Hemisphere into Polynesia. Also, Joseph F. Smith said the Maories are Hagoth's people ("Polynesians") *Encyclopedia of Mormonism*, Ed. by Daniel H. Ludlow, MacMillan Publishing Company, New York, 1992; pp. 1110, 1111.

16. Nibley, Hugh, *Collected Works of Hugh Nibley*, Vol. 8, FARMS, Provo, Utah, 1988; pp. 395-402.

17. *Reexploring The Book of Mormon*, John W. Welch, Ed., Deseret Book, Salt Lake City, 1992; pp. 142-144. See also: "Mulek," *Encyclopedia of Mormonism*, Vol. 2, Daniel H. Ludlow, Ed., MacMillan Publishing, New York, 1992; p. 969. See also: Nibley, Hugh, *Collected Works of Hugh Nibley*, Vol. 8, FARMS, Provo, Utah, 1988; pp. 398-400. See also: Sorenson, John L., "The Mulekites," *Brigham Young University Studies*, 30/3, Summer 1990; Brigham Young University, Provo, Utah; pp. 6-22.

18. Mattson, Vernon W. Jr., *The Dead Sea Scrolls and Other Important Discoveries*, Buried Record Productions, Salt Lake City, 1988; pp. 53-57.

19. *Reexploring The Book of Mormon*, John W. Welch, Ed., Deseret Book, Salt Lake City, 1992; pp. 250-252.

20. Tvedtnes, John A., "King Benjamin and the Feast of Tabernacles," in *By Study and Also by Faith, Essays in Honor of Hugh W. Nibley*, Eds. John M. Lundquist and Stephen D. Ricks, Deseret Book and FARMS, Salt Lake City, 1990; 2:197-237. See also Welch, John W. and Stephen D. Ricks, Eds., *King Benjamin's Speech: That Ye May Learn Wisdom*, FARMS, Provo, Utah, 1998.

21. Griffith, Michael T., *Refuting the Critics: Evidences of The Book of Mormon's Authenticity*, Horizon Publishers, Bountiful, Utah, 1993; pp. 73-75; See also: West, Jack H., *Trial of the Stick of Joseph,* Sounds of Zion, Midvale, Utah, 1981; pp. 54, 55. See also: Widtsoe John A. and Franklin S. Harris, Jr., *Seven Claims of The Book of Mormon,* Deseret News Press, Salt Lake City, 1937; pp. 95, 96.

22. Chadwick, Jeffrey R., "Sariah in the Elephantine Papyri," *Journal of Book of Mormon Studies,* FARMS, Provo, Utah, Fall, 1993; pp. 196-200.

23. Hoskisson, Paul Y., "Alma as a Hebrew Name," *Journal of Book of Mormon Studies,* FARMS, Provo, Utah, Spring 1998; pp. 72, 73.

24. Widtsoe John A. and Franklin S. Harris, Jr., *Seven Claims of The Book of Mormon*, Deseret News Press, Salt Lake City, 1937; p. 52.

25. Harris, Franklin S. Jr., *The Book of Mormon: Messages and Evidences,* Deseret Book, Salt Lake City, 1961; p. 121. See also: Reynolds, George, *The Story of The Book of Mormon,* Henry C. Etten & Co., Chicago, 1888.

26. Nibley, Hugh, *Teachings of The Book of Mormon*, Fall Semester, Brigham Young University, 1988-1990, FARMS, Provo, Utah; p. 15.

27. The Copan Pyramid has a perimeter of 2,866 feet. (See Widtsoe John A. and Franklin S. Harris, Jr., *Seven Claims of The Book of Mormon*, Deseret News Press, Salt Lake City, 1937; pp. 69-70.) The Great Pyramid of Gisa in Egypt has a perimeter of 3,012 feet (*The World Book Encyclopedia, World Book*—Childcraft International, Inc., Chicago, 1981; p. 810. Thirteen acres equal 753 feet per side). Insides are designed in a similar manner to Egyptian pyramids (Widtsoe John A. and Franklin S. Harris, Jr., *Seven Claims of The Book of Mormon,* Deseret News Press, Salt Lake City, 1937; p. 70).

28. The Sun Pyramid in San Juan Teotihuacan is 770 feet per side. (*Ibid.* p. 72). The Cholula Pyramid is 1,440 feet per side (*Ibid.* p. 72).

29. *Pressing Forward with The Book of Mormon,* Welch, John W. and Melvin J. Thorne, Eds., FARMS, Provo, Utah, 1999; pp. 237-243.

30. Harris, Franklin S. Jr., *The Book of Mormon: Messages and Evidences,* Deseret Book, Salt Lake City, 1961; p. 127.

31. *Ibid.* pp. 81, 114.

32. Gorton, H. Clay, *The Legacy of the Brass Plates of Laban,* Horizon Publishers, Bountiful, Utah, 1994; pp. 288-290. See also: Tvedtnes, John A., *Isaiah Variants in The Book of Mormon,* FARMS, Provo, Utah, 1984.

33. West, Jack H., *Trial of the Stick of Joseph,* Sounds of Zion, Midvale, Utah, 1981; pp. 52, 53. Reynolds and Sjodahl, *Commentary on The Book of Mormon,* Vol. 4, Deseret Book, Salt Lake City, 1989; p. 285.

34. Sorenson, John L., "Fortifications in The Book of Mormon Account Compared with Mesoamerican Fortifications," *Warfare in The Book of Mormon,* Ricks, Stephen D. and William J. Hamblin, Eds., Salt Lake City, Deseret Book, 1990; pp. 429-457. See also: Welch, John W. and J. Gregory Welch, *Charting The Book of Mormon,* FARMS, Provo, Utah, 1999; Charts 136-143.

35. Hess, Wilford M., Daniel Fairbanks, John W. Welch, and Jonathan K. Driggs, "Botanical Aspects of Olive Culture Relevant to Jacob 5," *The Allegory of the Olive Tree: The Olive, the Bible and Jacob 5,* Deseret Book and FARMS, Provo, Utah, 1994; pp. 484-562.

36. Peterson, Daniel C., "Mounting Evidence for The Book of Mormon," *Ensign,* The Church of Jesus Christ of Latter-day Saints, Salt Lake City, January 2000; pp. 21, 22.

37. Griffith, Michael T., *Refuting the Critics: Evidences of The Book of Mormon's Authenticity,* Horizon Publishers, Bountiful, Utah, 1993; pp 47-48. See also: West, Jack H., *Trial of the Stick of Joseph,* Sounds of Zion, Midvale, Utah, 1981, pp. 72-75. See also: Mattson, Vernon W. Jr., *The Dead Sea Scrolls and Other Important Discoveries,* Buried Record Productions, Salt Lake City, 1988; p. 62.

38. "Ancient Mayan Ceremonial City Found in Jungles of Guatemala," *The Denver Post,* November 14, 1989.

39. Reynolds, George, *The Story of The Book of Mormon,* 3rd ed., Henry C. Etten & Co., Chicago, 1888; pp. 285-286. See also: Stuy, Brian H., Ed., Thatcher, Moses, *Collected Discourses,* Vol. 1, November 11, 1888, BHS Publishing, Burbank, California, 1992. See also: Farnsworth, Dewey, *Book of Mormon Evidences in Ancient America,* Deseret Book, Salt Lake City, 1953; pp. 164, 165. See also: Mattson, Vernon W. Jr., *The Dead Sea Scrolls and*

Other Important Discoveries, Buried Record Productions, Salt Lake City, 1988; p. 64.

40. Nibley, Hugh, *Collected Works of Hugh Nibley,* Vol. 6, Preface p. xv. FARMS, Provo, Utah, 1988; See also: Nibley, Hugh, *Teachings of The Book of Mormon,* Semester 4, Brigham Young University, Provo, Utah; p. 239.

41. *Pressing Forward with The Book of Mormon,* Welch, John W. and Melvin J. Thorne, Eds., FARMS, Provo, Utah, 1999; pp. 250, 251.

42. Hunter, Milton R., *Christ in Ancient America,* Deseret Book, Salt Lake City, 1959. See also: Hansen, L. Taylor, *He Walked the Americas*, Legend Press, Amherst, Wisconsin, 1997. See also: Farnsworth, Dewey, *The Americas Before Columbus,* Deseret Book, Salt Lake City, 1964; pp. 28-37. See also: Yorgason, Blaine M., Warren, Bruce W., Brown, Harold, *New Evidences of Christ in Ancient America,* Stratford Books, Provo, Utah, 1999.3.

43. O'Brien, T. J., *Fair Gods and Feathered Serpents*, Horizon Publishers, Bountiful, Utah, 1997; p. 96. See also: Hunter, Milton R. *Conference Report*, Church of Jesus Christ of Latter-day Saints, Salt Lake City, October 1954, p. 108.

44. O'Brien, T. J., *Fair Gods and Feathered Serpents*, Horizon Publishers, Bountiful, Utah, 1997; p. 214. See also: Mattson, Vernon W. Jr., *The Dead Sea Scrolls and Other Important Discoveries,* Buried Record Productions, Salt Lake City, 1988; p. 82.

45. Griffith, Michael T., *Refuting the Critics: Evidences of The Book of Mormon's Authenticity,* Horizon Publishers, Bountiful, Utah, 1993; pp. 30-35.

46. Garr, Arnold K., *Christopher Columbus, A Latter-day Saint Perspective,* Religious Studies Center, Brigham Young University, Provo, Utah; p. 47. See also: Mattson, Vernon W. Jr., *The Dead Sea Scrolls and Other Important Discoveries,* Buried Record Productions, Salt Lake City, 1988; p. 78.

47. West, Jack H., *Trial of the Stick of Joseph,* Sounds of Zion, Midvale, Utah, 1981; pp. 75-78. See also: Roberts, B. H., *New Witnesses for God, Vol. 2,* Deseret Book, Salt Lake City, 1951; p. 483. See also: Rich, Ben E., *The Book of Mormon, Scrapbook of Mormon Literature,* Henry C. Etten & Co., Chicago, 1913; pp. 38, 39.

48. O'Brien, T. J., *Fair Gods and Feathered Serpents,* Horizon Publishers, Bountiful, Utah, 1997. See also: Reynolds and Sjodahl, *Commentary on The Book of Mormon, Vol. 4;* Deseret Book, Salt Lake City, 1989; p. 267. Widtsoe John A. and Franklin S. Harris,

Jr., *Seven Claims of The Book of Mormon,* Deseret News Press, Salt Lake City, 1937; pp. 101-103.

49. O'Brien, T. J., *Fair Gods and Feathered Serpents,* Horizon Publishers, Bountiful, Utah, 1997; pp. 226, 227.

50. *Reexploring The Book of Mormon,* John W. Welch, Ed., Deseret Book, Salt Lake City, 1992; pp. 212-214. See also: Farnsworth, Dewey, *The Americas Before Columbus,* Deseret Book, Salt Lake City, 1964; pp. 38, 39.

51. West, Jack H., *Trial of the Stick of Joseph,* Sounds of Zion, Midvale, Utah, 1981; pp. 94, 95. See also: Nibley, Hugh, *Collected Works of Hugh Nibley, Vol. 8,* FARMS, Provo, Utah, 1988; pp. 111, 112.

52. Wirth, Diane E., *A Challenge to the Critics,* Horizon Publishers, Bountiful, Utah, 1986; pp. 52-56. See also: *Reexploring The Book of Mormon,* John W. Welch, Ed., Deseret Book, Salt Lake City, 1992; pp. 98-100.

53. West, Jack H., *Trial of the Stick of Joseph,* Sounds of Zion, Midvale, Utah, 1981; pp. 88-92.

54. Griffith, Michael T., *Refuting the Critics: Evidences of The Book of Mormon's Authenticity,* Horizon Publishers, Bountiful, Utah, 1993; p. 56. See also: Wirth, Diane E., *A Challenge to the Critics,* Horizon Publishers, Bountiful, Utah, 1986; pp. 58-64.

55. Griffith, Michael T., *Refuting the Critics: Evidences of The Book of Mormon's Authenticity,* Horizon Publishers, Bountiful, Utah, 1993; pp. 55, 56. See also: West, Jack H., Trial of the *Stick of Joseph,* Sounds of Zion, Midvale, Utah, 1981; p. 97.

56. Wirth, Diane E., *A Challenge to the Critics,* Horizon Publishers, Bountiful, Utah, 1986; pp 37-45. See also: *Pressing Forward with The Book of Mormon,* Welch, John W. and Melvin J. Thorne, Eds., FARMS, Provo, Utah, 1999; pp. 20-22.

57. Widtsoe, John A., *Handbook of the Restoration, A Selection of Gospel Themes Discussed by Various Authors; Also Other Items of Interest to Gospel Students,* Centennial Series, Zion's Printing and Publishing Co., Independence, Missouri, 1944; p. 240.

58. *Pressing Forward with The Book of Mormon,* Welch, John W. and Melvin J. Thorne, Eds., FARMS, Provo, Utah, 1999; pp. 248-252.

59. "The Testimony of Three Witnesses," The Book of Mormon, The Church of Jesus Christ of Latter-day Saints, Salt Lake City, 1981.

60. Anderson, Richard Lloyd, *Investigating The Book of Mormon Witnesses*, Deseret Book, Salt Lake City, 1981; pp. 74, 75. See also: West, Jack H., *Trial of the Stick of Joseph,* Sounds of Zion, Midvale, Utah, 1981; pp. 26, 27.

61. Anderson, Richard Lloyd, *Investigating The Book of Mormon Witnesses,* Deseret Book, Salt Lake City, 1981; p. 90.

62. *Ibid.* pp. 57-60.

63. *Ibid.* pp. 62, 63. See also: Maxwell, Neal A., *Ensign,* The Church of Jesus Christ of Latter-day Saints, Salt Lake City, January 1997; p. 41.

64. Anderson, Richard Lloyd, *Investigating The Book of Mormon Witnesses,* Deseret Book, Salt Lake City, 1981; p 117.

65. "The Testimony of Eight Witnesses," The Book of Mormon, The Church of Jesus Christ of Latter-day Saints, Salt Lake City, 1981.

66. Anderson, Richard Lloyd, *Investigating The Book of Mormon Witnesses,* Deseret Book, Salt Lake City, 1981; pp. 30-32, 26, 27. See also: "Visitations of Moroni," *Encyclopedia of Mormonism, Vol. 2, ed.* by Daniel H. Ludlow, MacMillan Publishing Company, New York, 1992.

67. Anderson, Richard Lloyd, *Investigating The Book of Mormon Witnesses,* Deseret Book, Salt Lake City, 1981; pp 24, 25.

68. *Ibid.* pp 28-29.

69. *Ibid.* pp 22-24.

70. *Ibid.* p. 133.

7
Temples

The temples of The Church of Jesus Christ of Latter-day Saints are different from chapels or meetinghouses. Similar to ancient temples, the modern-day temples are built for the purpose of performing sacred ordinances. Only faithful members of the Church are granted permission to enter.

Soon after the Logan Temple was dedicated in 1884, federal marshals showed up at the door demanding access to all the records. Brother Samuel Roskelley, the temple recorder, denied them such access after which they said they would burn the temple down or even destroy it entirely if their demand was not granted.

Brother Roskelley became worried and spent the next eight hours at home in constant prayer. The next day when he reached the front door of the temple, there stood two giant men dressed in complete armor, with headdresses, breast plates and spears. They gave him a friendly nod as he entered the temple. He saw other such men inside. He asked who they were and they responded that they were Nephite warriors who had come in answer to Brother Roskelley's prayers. They told him not to worry as they would not allow the temple to be defiled or the records to be destroyed in any way.[1]

The day before the dedication of the Logan Temple, Bishop Henry Ballard was busy writing recommends for all the members of his ward who wished to attend the dedication. Two elderly gentlemen walked down the streets of Logan and approached Bishop Ballard's two daughters. One of them placed a newspaper in the hands of Ellen, age eight, and told her to take it directly to her father and not to lose it.

When Bishop Ballard's wife wanted to see the paper, Ellen said she had to give it to her father and no one else. She then entered the room and gave it to Bishop Ballard. The newspaper, *The Newbury Weekly News,* had been printed in Bishop Ballard's English birth place on Thursday, May 15, 1884, and reached his hands May, 18, 1884—three days later. He knew that there was no earthly means that the paper could have reached Logan, Utah in three days. It had recently taken the family twenty-six weeks to immigrate to Utah from Newbury.

As he examined the paper Bishop Ballard noticed there was one page devoted to the writings of a reporter of the paper who had gone on vacation and, among other places, had visited an old cemetery. The curious inscriptions led him to write what he found on the tombstones. He included names, birth dates, and death dates. The old cemetery was the same one where the Ballard family had been buried for generations. The paper contained about sixty names of dead relatives and acquaintances of the Ballards.

President Merrill, the president of the temple, told Brother Ballard: "That was two of the three Nephites who brought the paper to you, for it could come in no other way in so short a time. It is meant for you to do the temple work for these people."[2] Descendants of Henry Ballard later went to Newbury, England and verified that the paper received in Logan by Bishop Ballard was, in fact, printed in Newbury three days before it was given to him.

The Bible Dictionary says: "Whenever the Lord has had a people on the earth who would obey his word, they have been commanded to build temples in which the ordinances of the gospel and other spiritual manifestations that pertain to exaltation and eternal life may be administered."[3] Building and properly using a temple is one of the signs of the true Church.

The word "temple" means House of the Lord. Temples are where families are sealed together, where the Holy Ghost is manifest with power, where gifts of the Spirit are received in abundance, where the pure in heart may visit and receive personal revelations, and where God manifests himself to his children. Temples are the link between mankind and heaven and it has been said that heaven is one vast temple without walls. President Spencer W. Kimball said, "If you understood the ordinances of the House of the Lord, you would crawl on your hands and knees for thousands of miles in order to receive them."[4]

The Bible mentions several specific temples. The Garden of Eden was a prototype for temples on the earth.[5] Moses was commanded to build a tabernacle—a mobile sanctuary where he went to commune with God (Exodus 25-27). Solomon was directed by the Lord to design and build a great temple that required 180,000 workers to construct. It was the religious and political focal point for the Kingdom of Israel (1 Kings 6-8).

The Temple of Zerubbabel stood on the site of Solomon's Temple for over 500 years.[6] The Temple of Herod was built on the same site before the birth of Christ. The Savior learned and taught there. One of the reasons the Savior was crucified was because of his prophecy that the temple would be destroyed. That is exactly what happened forty years after his death when not one stone of the temple stood on another.[7]

In The Book of Mormon, we read of three principal temples: the Temple of Nephi, patterned after Solomon's Temple (2 Nephi 5:16); the Temple of Zarahemla (Mosiah 1:18; 2:1) where King Benjamin gave his wonderful discourse, which is among the best in all of the Holy Scriptures (Mosiah 2-6); and the Temple of Bountiful where the resurrected Savior appeared and taught the people who survived the destruction that occurred when Jesus was crucified (3 Nephi 11:1).

These temples, however, are just the tip of the iceberg. Hugh W. Nibley said that in ancient times the world was covered with temples.[8] John A. Widtsoe stated that "all people of all ages have had temples in one form or another."[9]

The three principal ordinances performed in the temples today, as revealed to the Prophet Joseph Smith, are baptism for the dead, the holy endowment, and the sealing of families. Joseph was commanded by the Lord to build temples in order that God's children might receive these sacred ordinances. Joseph designed and built the Kirtland Temple and the Nauvoo Temple, although such ordinances did not actually take place in the Kirtland Temple. Joseph also designed the temples that will be built in Zion and Far West. Let us review these sacred ordinances individually in terms of evidence of their truthfulness by examining their remnants throughout the cultures of ancient people.

First, there is **baptism for the dead.** In the Bible Paul asked, when speaking of the resurrection: "Else what shall they do which are baptized for the dead, if the dead rise not at all? Why are they then baptized for the dead?" (1 Corinthians 15:29). Such scholars as Hugh Nibley and John Tvedtnes have written extensively about how baptism for the dead was practiced by Christians for up to four centuries after the resurrection of the Savior.[10] It was practiced by such groups as the Marcionites, an early Christian group;[11] Orthodox Christian groups;[12] Coptics, who even practice it today on occasion;[13] Ethiopian Christians, called Abyssinians;[14] and early

Catholics, as reported by Augustine and others.[15] It makes sense that the Lord would provide a way for every person who has ever lived on the earth to have a means to receive the holy ordinance of baptism, which is required in order to enter the kingdom of God (John 3:5 and Mark 16:16).

The second ordinance performed in the Temple of the Lord is the **holy endowment.** The word "endowment" means a permanent gift like those given to universities in the form of funds or money. In the temples today, as we make covenants with the Lord, he *endows* us with eternal blessings. Brigham Young said:

> Your endowment is to receive all those ordinances in the House of the Lord, which are necessary for you, after you have departed this life, to enable you to walk back to the presence of the Father, passing the angels who stand as sentinels, being enabled to give them the key words, the signs and tokens, pertaining to the Holy Priesthood, and gain your eternal exaltation.[16]

In certain recently discovered ancient texts, we read that "Jesus asks that the twelve and the women disciples surround him so he can teach them the mysteries of God. What then follows in the text is a discussion of signs, seals and how to pass by the guardians at the veils to the presence of God"[17] In latter-day revelation we are told that angels serve as guardians along the way to exaltation (*D&C* 132:19) .

The third purpose served in the temple is the **sealing of families** for eternity. In the Garden of Eden the Lord told Adam and Eve that they should cleave unto each other and be one flesh (Genesis 2:24). Their marriage was performed by the Lord even before death came into the world. This alone indicates the eternal nature of marriage. Paul said, "Nevertheless neither is the man without the woman, neither the woman without the man, in the Lord." (1 Corinthians 11:11). Jesus gave Peter the keys to bind on earth that which will be bound or sealed in heaven (Matthew 16:19).

The Nag Hammadi Codices indicate that for 400 years after the crucifixion of Jesus Christ, the Gnostics, a Christian group who dwelled in Egypt, performed ordinances to seal families together for eternity. These were performed in a room called the "bridal chamber," which was surrounded with mirrors.[18] The sealing rooms in modern-day temples generally have mirrors on opposite sides so we may visualize how our ancestry and our posterity go on forever in the eternities.

Over the past 150 years, eighteen sets of ancient gold plates have been found in Europe and in the Middle East. All of these talk of the Tree of Life as well as a veil between heaven and earth where one must give signs and answers in order to pass through.[19] The temples of ancient civilizations in China, Japan, Siam, Africa, Egypt, Fiji, India, Israel and England had many commonalities including sacred and secret rituals, ceremonial ablutions or washings, and anointings with oil. Also new names were given to patrons, rebirth rituals were conducted, and the creation of the world was discussed. Ritual combat was symbolized depicting the conflict between good and evil, and light and darkness. Special garments were given, and there were sacred places for coronation of kings and queens.[20]

Documents recently found among the Dead Sea Scrolls and at other locations indicate that for two centuries before and after Jesus Christ, certain religious groups practiced rituals that included encounters with angels and guides, anointing patrons, and the receiving of celestial robes. Teaching about the use of secret names and tokens took place along with passing through the temple veil into the presence of God. Revelations of the secrets of creation and the exaltation and deification of the individuals were presented. Ascension into various levels of heaven representing different degrees of glory was a part of the ceremony. The necessity of moral purity was presented. Marriage for eternity was performed. All of the ceremonies were conducted in secrecy.[21]

Ancient papyri show that Egyptian temple worship included the traditional initiation of washing, clothing, and anointing patrons. By entering the temple itself, patrons would receive instructions on returning to the presence of God. In the temple, all would move from room to room, which symbolized increasing understanding and progress.[22]

Hugh Nibley said: "Plainly, the early Christians had something close to what we would call an endowment."[23] Dr. Nibley and other Church scholars have written about prayer circles that took place for several hundred years in the early Christian church.[24] Several early Christian documents teach that Adam was instructed by Peter, James and John.[25] Church scholars have also written extensively about such things as signs, tokens, and names in ancient temples.[26]

These are also apparent in many ancient statues in the Louvre Museum in Paris and in ancient Egyptian paintings.

Some people say there are remote resemblances of certain rituals in our temples and the rituals of Free Masons. These resemblances are extremely faint but are due to the fact that some Masonic symbols were passed down to them from the period of the Temple of Solomon.[27]

During the endowment ordinances, white clothing is worn as was prophesied by John in the Book of Revelation (3:5; 4:4; 6:11; 7:9). Clothing is the same for everyone who attends the temple, which depicts absolute equality in the House of the Lord.

In the initial part of the endowment ceremony, we covenant to wear the holy temple garment. There is abundant evidence of the importance of the garment in the eyes of God. In the Garden of Eden, the Lord made coats of skins for Adam and Eve (Genesis 3:21). These garments served as a spiritual and physical protection and were worn by the prophets who came after Adam and were his descendants. Adam's garments were a symbol of authority and were said to smell of paradise.[28] Ancient documents mention that Adam's garments were passed down through Enoch and Noah, then to Abraham and Isaac. Jacob purchased the holy garment from Esau, his brother, which garment was a symbol of the birthright.[29] Jacob gave the garment and birthright to his son Joseph.[30]

The "coat of many colors" worn by Joseph should actually be translated as "an upper garment in which figures are woven."[31] According to these ancient documents, this was Adam's very garment. After Joseph's brothers sold him to the Midianites going to Egypt, they dipped the garment in goat's blood and took it to their father Jacob to prove Joseph was dead. Although Jacob was blind, he knew the garment was Joseph's because of the smell of paradise and because of the marks or cuts in it.[32]

In the Old Testament the temple garment is mentioned in several scriptures. ". . . the holy garments for Aaron the priest, and the garments of his sons, to minister in the priest's office. And they came, every one whose heart stirred him up, and every one whom his spirit made willing to the work of the tabernacle and for the holy garment" (Exodus 35:19-21). In recent years, many mummies have been discovered with what is believed to be a religious garment with certain markings next to their skin.[33]

Archeologists and church scholars have written about ancient veils with marks of the square and the compass.[34] Ancient temple architecture was based on the square and the circle.[35]

The design and purpose of temple garments and temple clothing was specifically revealed to the Prophet Joseph Smith.

Some of the Christian priests' vestments today, such as the robes and aprons, are worn as vestiges of ancient temple dress. These were originally worn by Christian bishops and priests around 400 A.D., who, longing to retain temple rites, transferred them to non-temple ceremonies.[36]

The Savior gave Peter the power to seal in heaven that which is sealed on earth. Today we have that same power in the temples around the world. These temples are most sacred, as evidenced by the fact that at the completion and dedication of the first latter-day temple in Kirtland, Ohio, great spiritual experiences were manifest. Several persons saw the Savior whose countenance was above the brightness of the sun. His eyes were as a flame of fire and under his feet was a paved work of pure gold. Many saw angels. Hundreds heard great rushing winds and saw tongues of flames as if the temple were in a spiritual fire.[37] The dedicatory prayer was heard miles away.[38]

Christopher Columbus, John Wesley (who founded the Methodist Church), George Washington, and 100 other eminent men, including the Founding Fathers of this country and the signers of the Declaration of Independence, appeared to Wilford Woodruff for two days and two nights in the St. George Temple. They were requesting that their temple ordinances be performed for them.[39]

Moroni dedicated the site for the temple in Manti, Utah, some 1,600 years ago.[40] Brigham Young pointed precisely to where the St. George Temple should be built. It was in a swampland, rather than on a hill, and many believed that President Young must have been mistaken. He stated that the spot had been dedicated by ancient Book of Mormon prophets.[41] In 1881, William McBride, who was an ordained patriarch, quoted Joseph Smith as saying that Moroni dedicated the temple sites of Nauvoo, Jackson County, Kirtland, and others that we know not of as yet.[42]

Life's purpose is to return to our Heavenly Father as his children. The difficult journey is made lighter by having access to the temple.[43] Today we have more than 100 temples around the world that have been constructed in fulfillment of the restoration of the fulness of the Gospel. These temples and the work that goes on in them are additional evidence of the truthfulness of the Church.

Notes:

1. Olsen, Nolan Porter, *Logan Temple the First 100 Years,* Keith W. Watkins and Sons, Providence, Utah, 1978; pp. 171, 172.
2. Bennett, Archibald F., *Saviors on Mount Zion,* Deseret Sunday School Union Board, Salt Lake City, 1950, Ch. 43. See also: Olsen, Nolan Porter, *Logan Temple the First 100 Years*, Keith W. Watkins and Sons, Providence, Utah, 1978; pp. 153-155.
3. Bible Dictionary, The Church of Jesus Christ of Latter-day Saints, Salt Lake City, 1981; p. 781.
4. Ehat, Andrew F., "Who Shall Ascend into the Hill of the Lord?" *Temples of the Ancient World,* Parry, Donald W., Ed., Deseret Book and FARMS, Salt Lake City, 1984; p. 59.
5. Parry, Donald W., "Garden of Eden: Prototype Sanctuary," *Temples of the Ancient World,* Parry, Donald W., Ed., Deseret Book and FARMS, Salt Lake City, 1984; pp. 126-147.
6. Bible Dictionary, The Church of Jesus Christ of Latter-day Saints, Salt Lake City, 1981; pp. 783, 784.
7. *Ibid.* pp. 781-783.
8. Nibley, Hugh W., "Abraham's Temple Drama," *The Temple in Time and Eternity,* Parry Donald W. and Stephen D. Ricks, Eds., FARMS, Provo, Utah, 1999; p. 8.
9. Widtsoe, John A., "Temple Worship," *Utah Genealogical and Historical Magazine 12,* April 1921; p. 52.
10. Nibley, Hugh, *Mormonism and Early Christianity,* Deseret Book and FARMS, Salt Lake City, 1987; pp. 100-167. See also: Tvedtnes, John A., "Baptism for the Dead in Early Christianity," *The Temple in Time and Eternity,* Parry Donald W. and Stephen D. Ricks, Eds., FARMS, Provo, Utah, 1999; pp. 55-78.
11. Tvedtnes, John A., "Baptism for the Dead in Early Christianity," *The Temple in Time and Eternity*, Parry Donald W. and Stephen D. Ricks, Eds., FARMS, Provo, Utah, 1999; pp. 56, 57.
12. *Ibid.* pp. 57-59.
13. *Ibid.* pp. 67, 68.
14. *Ibid.* pp. 71, 72.
15. Nibley, Hugh, *Mormonism and Early Christianity*, Deseret Book and FARMS, Salt Lake City, 1987; pp. 141, 142.

16. Nibley, Hugh W., "On the Sacred and the Symbolic," *Temples of the Ancient World,* Parry, Donald W., Ed., Deseret Book and FARMS, Salt Lake City, 1984; pp. 537, 538. See also: *Journal of Discourses,* Latter-day Saints Book Depot, London, England, 1886; 2:31.

17. Tvedtnes, John A., "Temple Prayer in Ancient Times," *The Temple in Time and Eternity,* Parry Donald W. and Stephen D. Ricks, Eds., FARMS, Provo, Utah, 1999; p. 88.

18. Mattson, Vernon W. Jr., *The Dead Sea Scrolls and Other Important Discoveries,* Buried Record Productions, Salt Lake City, 1988; p. 41. See also: Seaich, Eugene, *Mormonism, the Dead Sea Scrolls and the Nag Hammadi Texts,* Sounds of Zion, Midvale, Utah, 1999; p. 13. See also: *The Nag Hammadi Library,* Robinson, James M., Ed., Harper, San Francisco, 1990; p. 151. See also: Cowan, Richard O., "Sacred Temples Ancient and Modern," *The Temple in Time and Eternity*, Parry Donald W. and Stephen D. Ricks, Eds., FARMS, Provo, Utah, 1999; p. 108.

19. Griggs, Wilfred, "Know Your Religion" seminars (author's notes, 1995).

20. Ricks Stephen D. and John J. Sroka, "King, Coronation, and Temple: Enthronement Ceremonies in History," *Temples of the Ancient World,* Parry, Donald W., Ed., Deseret Book and FARMS, Salt Lake City, 1984; pp. 236-271.

21. Hamblin, William J., "Temple Motifs in Jewish Mysticism," *Temples of the Ancient World*, Parry, Donald W., Ed., Deseret Book and FARMS, Salt Lake City, 1984; p. 463.

22. Cowan, Richard O., "Sacred Temples Ancient and Modern," *The Temple in Time and Eternity,* Parry Donald W. and Stephen D. Ricks, Eds., FARMS, Provo, Utah, 1999; pp. 106, 107.

23. Nibley, Hugh W., "On the Sacred and the Symbolic," *Temples of the Ancient World*, Parry, Donald W., Ed., Deseret Book and FARMS, Salt Lake City, 1984; p. 536.

24. Tvedtnes, John A., "Temple Prayer in Ancient Times," *The Temple in Time and Eternity,* Parry Donald W. and Stephen D. Ricks, Eds., FARMS, Provo, Utah, 1999; pp. 79-98. See also: Nibley, Hugh, *Mormonism and Early Christianity,* Deseret Book and FARMS, Salt Lake City, 1987; pp. 45-99.

25. Nibley, Hugh, *Temple and Cosmos,* Deseret Book and FARMS, Salt Lake City, 1992; pp. 300-303.

26. *Ibid.* pp. 59-61.

27. Ballard, Melvin J., *General Conference Reports,* The Church of Jesus Christ of Latter-day Saints, Salt Lake City, October 1913.
28. Tvedtnes, John A., "Priestly Clothing in Bible Times," *Temples of the Ancient World,* Parry, Donald W., Ed., Deseret Book and FARMS, Salt Lake City, 1984; p. 657. See also: Nibley, Hugh, *Temple and Cosmos,* Deseret Book and FARMS, Salt Lake City, 1992; p. 132.
29. Ricks, Stephen D., "The Garment of Adam in Jewish, Muslim, and Christian Tradition," *Temples of the Ancient World*, Parry, Donald W., Ed., Deseret Book and FARMS, Salt Lake City, 1984; pp. 711, 712.
30. Tvedtnes, John A., "Priestly Clothing in Bible Times," *Temples of the Ancient World,* Parry, Donald W., Ed., Deseret Book and FARMS, Salt Lake City, 1984; pp. 657, 658. See also: Nibley, Hugh, "Lecture 9—The Shabako Stone," *Ancient Documents and the Pearl of Great Price,* Robert Smith and Robert Smythe, Eds., FARMS, Provo, Utah, 1986.
31. Tvedtnes, John A., "Priestly Clothing in Bible Times," *Temples of the Ancient World,* Parry, Donald W., Ed., Deseret Book and FARMS, Salt Lake City, 1984; p. 658.
32. Nibley, Hugh, *Temple and Cosmos,* Deseret Book and FARMS, Salt Lake City, 1992; p. 132.
33. *Ibid.* pp. 107-112.
34. *Ibid.* p. 111. Nibley, Hugh, "On the Sacred and the Symbolic," *Temples of the Ancient World*, Parry, Donald W., Ed., Deseret Book and FARMS, Salt Lake City, 1984; pp. 574, 575.
35. Ibid. pp. 139-171.
36. Tvedtnes, John A., "Priestly Clothing in Bible Times," *Temples of the Ancient World,* Parry, Donald W., Ed., Deseret Book and FARMS, Salt Lake City, 1984; p. 694.
37. *History of the Church,* The Deseret Book Company, Salt Lake City, 1980; 2:379-436. See also: Backman, Milton V. Jr., "Establish a House of Prayer, a House of God: The Kirtland Temple," *The Prophet Joseph,* Porter, Larry C. and Susan Easton Black, Eds., Deseret Book Company, Salt Lake City; pp. 208-225. See also: *The Temple in Time and Eternity,* Parry Donald W. and Stephen D. Ricks, Eds., FARMS, Provo, Utah, 1999; p. 109.
38. As told to the author by a guide at the Kirtland Temple.
39. Journal of Discourses, 19:229. See also: Benson, Ezra Taft, *Teachings of Ezra Taft Benson*, Bookcraft, Salt Lake City, 1988; p. 604.

40. *Book of Mormon Symposium Series,* Monte S. Nyman and Charles D. Tate, Jr., Eds., Religious Studies Center, Brigham Young University, Provo, Utah, 1988-1995; p. 244.
41. *Encyclopedia of Mormonism,* edited by Daniel H. Ludlow, Macmillan Publishing Company, New York, 1992 p. 1,452.
42. *Book of Mormon Symposium Series,* Monte S. Nyman and Charles D. Tate, Jr., Eds., Religious Studies Center, Brigham Young University, Provo, Utah, 1988-1995; p. 244.
43. Lundquist, John M., "What is Reality?" *Temples of the Ancient World,* Parry, Donald W., Ed., Deseret Book and FARMS, Salt Lake City, 1984; p. 633.

8
Miracles

From the time of the creation of the world, miracles have provided evidence of the true Church of God on the earth. As two prophets wrote in The Book of Mormon:

Have miracles ceased? Behold I say unto you, Nay; neither have angels ceased to minister unto the children of men. For it is by faith that miracles are wrought; and it is by faith that angels appear and minister unto men (Moroni 7:29, 37). And if there were miracles wrought then, why has God ceased to be a God of miracles and yet be an unchangeable Being? And Behold, I say unto you he changeth not; if so he would cease to be God; and he ceaseth not to be God, and is a God of miracles (Mormon 9:19).

When some of the Saints were in Independence, Missouri in 1833, a mob approached and said that after twenty-four hours, any Mormons remaining on the south side of the Missouri River would be bull whipped. All of the member families crossed over the river except three: the Higbee, Lewis, and Rollins families. They did not have the fifty-cent fee for the ferry to cross over.

Brother Higbee suggested they drop fishing lines into the river, believing they might catch some fish to give to the ferry captain for passage. One of them soon caught a fourteen-pound, two-foot catfish. When Brother Higbee cut it open to clean it, with all three families watching, he found inside the fish three bright, shiny, silver half-dollars, the exact amount needed to pay for ferry passage for the three families.[1]

In 1834, a group of about 200 men were involved in what was called Zion's Camp. They accompanied the Prophet Joseph on an excursion to help the Saints in Missouri. They camped one night at a tiny stream called Fishing River in western Missouri. A report came to them that a mob of several hundred men was going to attack them soon. Many were afraid but Joseph instructed them to remember that they had gone to that place in response to God's commandment. They were there on the Lord's errand and they had the right to his protection, and protect them he would.

A small cloud soon appeared on the horizon, which unrolled like a huge, black scroll. It grew rapidly until the thunderhead darkened the whole sky. Giant hailstones came out of nowhere. Great winds bellowed and flashes of lightning were everywhere. The heavens had opened. The torrent of rain was so massive that within thirty minutes, the stream, which was usually about a foot or two deep and five or six feet across, became a raging torrent forty feet wide and thirty to forty feet deep. The mob was turned away and some of their leaders later admitted that only the power of the Almighty himself had saved the Mormons. Zion's Camp was spared by this great miracle.[2]

When the word "miracles" is mentioned, people think of Old Testament times like Moses parting the Red Sea (Exodus 14); manna from heaven, which was provided to the children of Israel for 40 years (Exodus 16); and Daniel surviving after being thrown in the lions' den (Daniel 6). Then there was Shadrach, Meshach and Abed-nego's experience of being cast into the fiery furnace (Daniel 3); David, the young shepherd, conquering Goliath (1 Samuel 17); Elijah and then Elisha raising children from the dead (I Kings 17; 2 Kings 4); and Enoch's moving mountains and changing the course of rivers (Moses 7).

Perhaps when you think of miracles you think of the life of Jesus Christ when he changed the water to wine (John 2); when he fed 5,000 on one occasion (Mark 8) and 4,000 on another (Mark 6) with a few loaves of bread and fishes; and when he caused the blind to see, the lame to walk, the leprous to be healed, devils to be cast out. There was also the time when he raised a twelve-year-old girl from the dead (Mark 5); when he raised a widow's son from the dead (Luke 7); when he commanded Lazarus to arise and come forth from the tomb after he had been dead for four days (John 11); and maybe you think of the Atonement in the Garden of Gethsemane and the resurrection from the tomb which, together, are the greatest of all miracles.

After Christ's ascension into heaven there were additional miracles. Peter and John healed the lame (Acts 3); Peter raised a woman from the dead (Acts 9); and angels freed Peter from prison on two occasions (Acts 5, 12). On the day of Pentecost many spoke in tongues, heard rushing winds, saw tongues of fire and were filled with the spirit (Acts 2). Paul had a great vision on the road to Damascus (Acts 9); he later cast out devils (Acts 16); blessed others to speak in tongues (Acts 19); and was visited by angels (Acts 27).

There were great miracles among the ancient peoples in The Book of Mormon. The Brother of Jared saw the finger of Jesus Christ touch small stones turning them into light for the barges. He then saw the body of the Savior 2,200 years before Jesus came to the earth (Ether 3). "The Brother of Jared said unto the mountain Zerin, Remove—and it was removed" (Ether 12:30).

Because of jealousy, Nephi's brothers tied him to the masthead of their ship. A great storm came up and the ship nearly sank. This frightened Laman and Lemuel so they released him. Then the Lord calmed the storm as a result of Nephi's prayers (1 Nephi 18). Alma and Amulek were put in prison when the walls were suddenly broken in two and came tumbling down. Those around them were killed but Alma and Amulek's lives were spared (Alma 14).

The lives of 2,000 stripling youths who were led into battle by Helaman were miraculously saved from suffering death at the hands of their enemies, the Lamanites, because of the covenants they had made with the Lord (Alma 56). Helaman recounts a marvelous story about Nephi and Lehi being encircled by flames of fire and not injured. Angels came down and ministered to them and to 300 people (Helaman 5).

Nephi, the grandson of Helaman, cast out devils and raised his brother from the dead (3 Nephi 7). When Jesus Christ appeared to inhabitants in America, he healed the sick and caused the blind to see (3 Nephi 17). After the ascension of Jesus Christ:

> There were great and marvelous works wrought by the disciples of Jesus, insomuch that they did heal the sick, and raise the dead, and cause the lame to walk, and the blind to receive their sight, and the deaf to hear; and all manner of miracles did they work among the children of men. (4 Nephi 5).

Great miracles have occurred since the Restoration of the Gospel with literally thousands of examples. When the Saints were settled in Nauvoo, Illinois, many of them became very sick. The Prophet Joseph Smith and others crossed the Mississippi River to Montrose, Iowa where many of the members were ill and suffering greatly. He went to visit Elijah Fordham who was dying. Joseph commanded him in the name of Jesus Christ to be made well. Elijah got up from his bed, ate a bowl of bread and milk and then accompanied Joseph into the street, where they healed others.[3]

On another occasion Joseph was introduced to Elsa Johnson, who had a lame arm. He said, "Woman, in the name of the Lord Jesus Christ, I command thee to be whole." She stretched out her arm and it was instantly made well.[4]

David Whitmer asked his father if he could go to Pennsylvania at the request of his friend, Oliver Cowdery, to help a man named Joseph Smith, who was translating an ancient record. His father said David would first have to plow the family's field, then fertilize his sister's. He said these tasks would take a few days, after which they would talk about his going. When David went to the field in the morning, half of it was already plowed and he finished it in one day. When he went to his sister's field, it had already been fertilized by three unknown men.[5]

During an eight week period in Kirtland, Ohio in early 1836, Latter-day Saints saw heavenly beings in Church meetings on at least ten occasions. Many saw angels. On five different occasions the Savior Jesus Christ appeared and on one occasion, Heavenly Father also appeared. At the dedication of the Kirtland Temple, some saw the face of Jesus Christ and many saw angels. Hundreds of others heard rushing winds and saw tongues of fire.[6]

When the Saints moved to the Salt Lake Valley they planted their crops and settled in. The next spring, millions of crickets came out of the canyons and began eating the sprouts and seedlings. These crops were the Saints' only means of survival. The infestation was like one of the plagues of the Old Testament. After the Saints' fervent prayers in which they pleaded for help, thousands of seagulls appeared out of nowhere and ate the crickets.[7]

The Apostle Matthew Cowley was visiting a small village in New Zealand where the sisters in the Relief Society were preparing the body of a Church member who had died. Brother Cowley and another priesthood holder laid their hands on his head and commanded him to rise, which he did! Elder Cowley on another occasion, completely healed a child who was born deaf, dumb, and blind. On still another occasion he gave a young blind child his eyesight.[8]

Are these miracles simply coincidences or psychological phenomena as some would have us believe? I have seen a number of occasions where an X-ray shows an abnormal growth or a broken bone one day and on the next, following a priesthood blessing, the growth has disappeared or the broken bone has been healed.

Some ask about the faith healings of other churches or miracles performed outside the Church. No doubt, some of them are real. The blessings of our Heavenly Father are not reserved solely for Latter-day Saints. There are millions of good, honorable, faithful people in the world who are greatly blessed by the light of Christ, by the power of the Holy Ghost, and by our Heavenly Father.

I have personally witnessed hundreds of miracles in my lifetime and have been greatly blessed by them. The greatest miracles are the simplest. Look at the stars and the vastness of the universe. Look at the birth of a baby. Look at a beautiful flower. Look at the miraculous parts of the human body. Are not all of these great miracles? Is not life itself a great miracle?

Every person is given gifts by the Spirit of God. Some of these gifts, which are miracles themselves, are listed in the forty-sixth section of the Doctrine & Covenants. They are also listed in The Book of Mormon in Moroni chapter ten, and in the Bible in First Corinthians chapter twelve. We should prayerfully ask which specific gifts we have been given.

Other than our sun, the closest star to us is Alpha Centauri, which is more than four light years away. As far as our scientific principles teach us, the fastest anything can travel is the speed of light. Nothing we know of can travel faster than this. This means that if heaven were on the closest star, it would take our prayers at least four years to reach heaven and another four years for us to receive an answer. If you have ever received an answer to prayer in less than eight years, isn't that a true miracle?

Perhaps the greatest miracle of all, next to the Atonement and the Resurrection of the Savior, is simply feeling the Spirit or watching the Spirit change someone's heart. Is that not a wonderful miracle? The Spirit is often felt while listening or singing uplifting music, when listening to the testimonies of others, or when softening our heart and truly humbling ourselves before the Lord. It changes your life and that of others; and it changes mine.

I have found that in missionary interviews, the *good* missionaries talk about obedience to the mission rules, working hard, getting along with their companions, loving the people, and wanting to baptize converts and reactivate those who are less active. These missionaries see many miracles. I have found, however, that the *great* missionaries often talk first about the Savior, the Atonement, and striving to conform their will to Heavenly Father's. Then they talk about trying to be good missionaries. They witness even greater miracles as they rely totally on the Lord and let the Spirit guide them in their work.

Whenever the Gospel is on the earth, miracles follow. Wherever there are faithful people who love God, the Lord will bless them. In truth, all blessings are miracles.

Notes:

1. "Mary Lightner, Autobiography," Milton Backman, Jr. and Keith W. Perkins, Eds., *Writings of Early Latter-day Saints and Their Contemporaries, Utah Genealogical and Historical Magazine,* 2nd Ed., Religious Studies Center, Provo, Utah, 1996.
2. Smith, Joseph, *History of the Church,* The Deseret Book Company, Salt Lake City, 1980; 2:103-105. See also: Philo Dibble's Narrative, Milton Backman, Jr. and Keith W. Perkins, Eds., *Writings of Early Latter-day Saints and Their Contemporaries, Utah Genealogical and Historical Magazine,* 2nd Ed., Religious Studies Center, Provo, Utah, 1996. See also: Elder Joseph F. McGregor, *General Conference Reports,* The Church of Jesus Christ of Latter-day Saints, Salt Lake City, 1880.
3. Smith, Joseph Fielding, *Church History and Modern Revelation,* The Council of the Twelve Apostles of The Church of Jesus Christ of Latter-day Saints, Salt Lake City, 1946. See also: Roberts, B.H., *Comprehensive History of The Church,* reprint Sonos Publishing Inc., Orem, Utah, 1991.
4. Smith, Lucy Mack, *History of Joseph Smith by His Mother, Revised and Enhanced,* Scot Facer Proctor and Maurine Jensen Proctor, Eds., Bookcraft, Salt Lake City, 1996; Chapter 41 notes.
5. Roberts, B. H., *New Witnesses for God,* Vol. II, Deseret News, Salt Lake City, p. 124.
6. *History of the Church,* The Deseret Book Company, Salt Lake City, 1980; 2:379-436. See also: Backman, Milton V. Jr., "Establish a House of Prayer, a House of God: The Kirtland Temple." *The Prophet Joseph,* Porter, Larry C. and Susan Easton Black, Eds., Deseret Book Company, Salt Lake City, 1988; pp. 208-225. See also: Cowan, Richard O., "Sacred Temples Ancient and Modern," *The Temple in Time and Eternity,* Parry, Donald W. and Stephen D. Ricks, Eds., FARMS, Provo, Utah, 1999; p. 109.

7.   Berrett, William E., *The Restored Church,* Deseret Book Company, Salt Lake City, 1964; pp. 284, 285.

8.   Cowley, Matthew, *Matthew Cowley Speaks,* Deseret Book, Salt Lake City, 1954; pp. 237-249.

9
Blessings

There is much good to be found in almost all churches. We invite everyone to bring their blessings from their other churches and see how The Church of Jesus Christ of Latter-day Saints can add to them. You will find great blessings that you cannot find elsewhere.

When I was about twelve years old my bishop announced that the home of Frank and Ida Stephenson had burned to the ground the previous night. They had no insurance to cover the costs of rebuilding the house. Everyone in the congregation gasped as they knew that the Stephensons, who were an older couple, had several months left to serve their mission, which, as I recall, was in Central America.

The bishop proposed that the ward rebuild their house without notifying Frank and Ida. He also suggested that since their home was so small, we should build it to double its previous size. I remember going night after night for several months with my father to help haul concrete, to measure floorboards, and to nail shingles to the roof.

When the Stephensons returned from their mission, their daughter picked them up at the train station and drove down the driveway through their small orchard to their new home. They looked up and asked what had happened. Their daughter then explained that their house had burned to the ground and the ward members had rebuilt their home. They then came inside and over 100 members from the ward were there to welcome them. I will always remember the feeling I had as they walked through the door.

One of the blessings of the Church is that we are a large *family*—Heavenly Father's family. We take care of each other and we always have friends, anywhere in the world. Whether you move from Alaska to Brazil, or from New Zealand to Sweden, you can immediately obtain the help you need from members of the Church. Sometimes they help you move in; sometimes they help you in adjusting and in providing you a full social life. There is an immediate bonding—an immediate friendship and closeness. You will also find identical and consistent truths and doctrines taught in the Church throughout the world.

Another blessing is **the fruits of the Gospel.** The Savior said: "By their fruits ye shall know them" (Matthew 7:20; 3 Nephi 14:20). From a number of studies, it appears that Mormons are the healthiest people in the world. A recent study by the UCLA Medical School concluded that Mormons live an average of seven to ten years longer than their peers.[1] Another study concluded that the incidence of cancer among Mormons is just fifty percent of the national average.[2]

The *Statistical Abstract of the United States* publishes information each year regarding health issues. It reports selected diseases state by state. Utah's population is approximately 70% Mormon and not all Mormons in Utah are active in the Church, which means the statistics cannot be separated according to the level of activity of members of the Church. In 1999, Utah ranked 49th among the 50 states in the incidence of heart disease; 50th in cancer; 49th in cerebrovascular diseases; 48th in chronic obstructive pulmonary diseases; and 42nd in diabetes. Overall, Utah ranked 50th of all the states in all the diseases considered.[3] The death rate per capita in Utah is 49th among all the states in the U.S. with Alaska with the lowest.[4] In births to unmarried women as a percentage of total births, Utah is in 50th place.[5] As expected, as to the total birth rate per capita, Utah is in first place.[6]

The *Statistical Abstract of the United States* also publishes selected information each year regarding issues of education by state. The most recent abstract shows that over the past 15 years, of the 50 states in the U.S., Utah has had the highest percentage of students in grades kindergarten through twelfth, which is 98%.[7] The percentage of persons 25 years old and older who have graduated from high school is 87%, second only in the U.S. to Alaska with 90%.[8] Utah's percentage of college graduates is also among the top few states.[8]

There are many Mormon congressmen, generals, and admirals. Mormons have been presidents of Rotary International, Lions International, the American Medical Association, the American Bankers Association, and hundreds of large corporations.[9] Many members of the Church have had a great influence in the world. For example, Philo Farnsworth invented television. Harvey Fletcher invented stereophonic sound. Both were Mormons.

The incidence of divorce among Mormons married in the temple is only 6% compared to 50% to 60% for non-Mormons. For Mormons not married in the temple, the divorce rate is about 30%.[10]

A third blessing for members of the Church is that we understand the *joy of service*. I added up the estimated hours of service for a typical ward of the Church in a given month, which included the bishopric, executive secretary, and clerks; Relief Society officers and teachers; elders quorum officers and teachers; high priests group leaders and teachers; Sunday School presidencies and teachers; young men's and young women's officers and teachers; Primary officers and teachers; music personnel; activities committees; librarians; stake officers in the ward; full-time and stake missionaries; home teachers and visiting teachers; and leaders of Boy Scouts and Cub Scouts. The total hours of service in a typical ward are approximately 3,000 hours per month. If family home evenings, family scripture study, and family service projects are counted, the total hours of service are well over 5,000 per month.

The Church provides great assistance when needed for natural disasters throughout the world. Recent examples of assistance rendered include Armenia, Russia, the Philippines, Guatemala, South America, and elsewhere. From 1995 through 1998, the Church gave $162 million and millions of man-hours in aid.[11] Over the past ten years the Church has shipped more than 27,000 tons of clothing, 16,000 tons of food, and 3,000 tons of medical and educational supplies and equipment to Heavenly Father's children in 146 countries.[12]

A man was caught up in a dream where he was taken into hell. He saw many tables filled with all kinds of food, e.g., turkey, dressing, yams, roast beef, salads, casseroles, pizza, hamburgers, hot fudge sundaes, chocolate cake, banana cream pie, and anything else anyone might desire. All the people, however, were crying. The man saw that they all had long spoons tied to their arms so they could not bend their elbows. They could dish up the food of their dreams, but could not get it to their mouths. He realized that this would surely be hell—to see but not be able to partake.

His dream then took him into heaven. He saw similar tables filled with food—everything imaginable. Here, though, he saw everyone smiling and laughing. He saw they, too, had long spoons tied to their arms and could not bend their elbows. However, here in heaven they were all feeding *each other*. He realized that this was surely heaven. The Church teaches us in a very real way how to serve and help each other.

A fourth example of blessings are those that come from **keeping the commandments.** A recently baptized couple came to me to see if I might help them figure out how to pay their tithing when they had a very tight budget. They just could not see how to fit it in. I reviewed their budget and agreed; their money was all committed before they earned it. There was no practical way they could pay tithing. I then promised them through the power of the priesthood that if they paid their tithing first, somehow they would have sufficient for their needs. The windows of heaven would open.

They looked at each other contemplating my words, then committed to pay their tithing first thing every payday. They had made covenants in the waters of baptism and they wanted to keep the Lord's commandments.

The next day this young man called me— excited. That morning his boss called him in to his office and told him that he had decided to give the young man a surprise—a ten-percent raise in pay! The Lord promises us everything if we exercise our faith and just give him back ten percent. If we do, he says that he will make certain we have sufficient for our needs (Malachi 3:10, 11).

The other commandments also have special blessings associated with them. For example, the Word of Wisdom says that if we abstain from the use of tobacco, alcohol, coffee, and tea, we will receive wisdom and great treasures of knowledge, even hidden treasures, along with the blessings of good health (D&C 89:18-21).

President Ezra Taft Benson promised us that if we attend the temple regularly, we will receive more personal revelation in our lives.[13] He also promised that if we read The Book of Mormon daily, "God will pour out a blessing hitherto unknown"[14] and he promised that as we diligently study modern revelation, our power to preach and teach will be magnified.[15] President Marion G. Romney promised that contention in our homes will diminish as we read The Book of Mormon together as families.[16] As we remain virtuous and clean, the Holy Ghost will be our constant companion (D&C 121:45, 46). In 1965 President David O. McKay promised us that if we faithfully hold family home evenings, our children will gain power "to choose righteousness and peace, and be assured an eternal place in the family circle of our Father."[17]

A fifth blessing of the Church is *revelation*. We have a modern-day prophet to guide us. There are many revelations that have been given through our prophets, just in the past few years. They include the revelation that the priesthood can be conferred upon all worthy men; the Proclamation to the World on the Family; the Testimony of the Apostles on the Living Christ; the building of numerous, smaller temples; the Perpetual Education Fund, counsel that we should obtain a year's supply of food and clothing and stay out of debt; and that Church members and the Church itself should be self-reliant. (For the Church itself to be self-reliant, there are more than 100 bishop's storehouses, 160 Church employment centers, sixty-five LDS Social Services offices, and hundreds of welfare projects, such as farms, ranches, dairies, factories etc.[18])

I was asked to speak at a Christian symposium, together with four other ministers. We were each asked to speak for twenty minutes about the doctrines and teachings of our respective churches. The minister from the United Church of Christ spoke first and said that he was unable to speak for twenty minutes about doctrines because their church had no doctrines. They had a one-page "Statement of Faith" pasted in the front of their hymn books, which said they believe in the Father, the Son and the Holy Spirit, and that they should be good people. After that, the members could believe anything they chose.

The minister from the Congregational Church stood up and said virtually the same thing: They had no doctrines in their church. He reported that he held a masters degree in theology and had studied the Bible for many years. He had decided that he was not comfortable leading a church that did not follow the Bible and he was looking for the true church with doctrinal teachings from the Bible.

The third minister was a woman who was a full-blooded Navajo. She said she was a minister from the United Methodist Church. She had tried to merge the Navajo religion with Christianity. She said that Methodist doctrine was very soft and she was not comfortable with this, so she also was looking for the truth.

A Catholic Priest then took his turn and said that the regret of his life was that the Pope had not allowed him to marry and have children. Then he said: "For the next twenty minutes, let me talk about the many other areas where I disagree with the Pope."

It was a privilege for me to speak about the restored Church of Jesus Christ, a modern-day prophet, the additional scriptures that we have, and Heavenly Father's plan of salvation.

As a sixth blessing, we have a revealed **understanding of the Bible as well as additional scriptures** to guide us that other churches do not have. We believe in the Bible that gives us glimpses of how the Church should be organized. It should have apostles (Ephesians 4:13), prophets (Ephesians 2:20), high priests (Hebrews 5:10), seventies (Luke 10:1), the Melchizedek Priesthood (Hebrews 6:20), and the Aaronic Priesthood (Hebrews 7:11).

The Bible teaches us important doctrines about the pre-mortal life in heaven (Jeremiah 1:5), the three kingdoms (1 Corinthians 15:40), paradise (Luke 23:43), spirit prison (I Peter 3:19), baptism for the dead (I Corinthians 15:29), revelation (Amos 3:7), the laying on of hands for the Gift of the Holy Ghost (Acts 8:17), sealing of families in heaven (Matthew 16:19), the spirit children of God (Romans 8:16), creation of man in the image of God (Genesis 1:27), and the potential to become as God is (Romans 8:17; Psalms 82:6).

To my knowledge, not one of the thousands of other Christian churches preaches even one of these doctrines. Yet, these teachings are all in the Bible. The Bible contains only part of the Gospel, however. That is the reason there are more than 20,800 Christian churches on the earth today, each with its own interpretation of the Bible.

In addition to the Bible we have The Book of Mormon to guide and comfort us. It was given to all of Heavenly Father's children as a second witness of Jesus Christ. As Bruce R. McConkie taught, the Bible explains the "what" and the "how" of the Gospel. *The Book of Mormon* explains the "why." It greatly clarifies the Gospel of Jesus Christ. We also have *The Doctrine and Covenants* and *The Pearl of Great Price* that give us additional revelations to direct and assist us in our lives and in the Savior's Church.

As a seventh blessing, we have **gifts of the priesthood and of the Spirit**. As members of the Church we may each receive a patriarchal blessing to use as a compass to direct us. Because we have the Holy Priesthood, we may also receive necessary holy ordinances, by the proper authority, in order for us to return to our Heavenly Father. These ordinances include baptism, the holy temple endowment, and eternal marriage. The gifts of the Spirit or gifts of the priesthood are among the few major topics that are described in all three scriptures: *The Doctrine and Covenants* (46:11-33), *The Book of Mormon* (Moroni 10:8-18), and the *Bible* (1 Corinthians 12:1-11).

To every person is given at least one gift (D&C 46:11). Some of the gifts that are mentioned include knowing by the Holy Ghost that Jesus Christ is the Son of God; gifts of wisdom, knowledge, healings, and faith to heal. Still other gifts are working miracles; prophesying; discerning spirits; speaking in tongues; interpreting tongues; discerning gifts; possessing great faith; beholding angels and ministering spirits; and teaching wisdom and knowledge by the Spirit. Which gifts have you been given? Different gifts may come to us at different times in our lives, depending on our needs.

A woman came to me to ask for a priesthood blessing because she had a lump in her body that the doctor thought was malignant. She was scheduled for surgery the following week. As I began to lay my hands on her head, she asked if I would also bless her husband through her. He was a not a member of the Church and would not let her attend church meetings. She just wanted his heart to be softened.

Through me, the Lord gave her the blessings that she requested. A few days later, when she went into surgery, the doctors found nothing—the tumor or growth had completely disappeared. The next month her husband began taking the missionary discussions. I recently saw him in the temple where he is now a regular temple worker.

As an eighth blessing we have the *Gift of the Holy Ghost.* In these troubled times of depression, suicide, drugs, abortion, alcoholism, divorce, materialism, wars, etc., we have the Holy Ghost to comfort us, to protect us, to teach us, and to be a witness to us of the truth. Most often the Spirit simply comes to us in a manner that makes us feel right, or feel at peace, or telling us what makes sense. In some cases, it comes as a powerful, spiritual witness.

Several years ago I was teaching a Sunday School lesson when I said I believe that all members of the Church have the privilege of receiving a spiritual witness through the Holy Ghost, at least once in their lives. This witness will tell them that Joseph Smith was a prophet of God, that The Book of Mormon is the word of God, and that the Church is true.

My mother happened to be visiting the class. Afterward, she felt a need to speak with me. That afternoon she told me she had never felt a witness of the truthfulness of the Gospel of which I had spoken. She said that she was fifty-five years old, had been a member of the Church all her life and knew the Church was true, because it just *felt* right. But she said she had never had a spiritual manifestation or feeling about it. She thought she would insult the Lord if she asked for a spiritual witness since she already knew the Church was true.

I explained to her how the Holy Ghost speaks to us in many different voices. Sometimes he speaks to our mind, other times to our heart. Sometimes, he speaks in a very still small voice, other times in a warm, wonderful feeling. I explained that since she felt that the Church was true, she *had* received a witness of the Spirit.

She understood my explanation. However, she said she would like to feel the warm feeling, the "burning in the bosom," just once in her life so she would know it to be a witness that the Church was true. I told her that she should go home, kneel down, and tell Heavenly Father what she told me. She should ask him for a witness of the Holy Ghost. The next week she called and said that her life had been changed. She was a different person. She had felt the witness of the Holy Ghost through her whole being.

When my son was in his first year of attendance at Brigham Young University, he arrived at his apartment late one night and found his roommate asleep. Since he had committed to one of his professors that he would read from The Book of Mormon every day, he walked quietly into the room without turning on the light, took his book and left. He sat on the floor of the dorm hallway and began to read. He noticed that no one was around, which was a rare moment in the dorm. After reading for awhile, he found a small closet filled with brooms, mops, and buckets. He went in, closed the door, and poured out his heart to Heavenly Father, asking for a spiritual witness of The Book of Mormon. He felt the Spirit descend on him, starting from the top of his head and proceeding down his body until it covered his feet. It was like a warm blanket completely covering him and telling him that the Book was the word of God.

As a ninth blessing, we have the ***plan of salvation.*** We know where we came from before this life, why we are here on the earth, and where we are going after this life. Because of this knowledge, we have an eternal perspective about death, afflictions, trials, and troubles. It gives us direction and comfort. We know that before this life, we all lived as spirits with our Heavenly Father in a pre-mortal existence. We were literally his spirit children. He taught us the importance of coming to earth. The reasons included gaining a mortal body in order to have eternal happiness, gaining experiences, being tried and tested to show that we will remain true to Heavenly Father, becoming loving people, and forming a family unit.

Heavenly Father knew that by blessing us with our agency to choose, we would inevitably sin and be unable to return to him unless an eternal redemption was made to pay for our sins. Our older brother, Jesus Christ, volunteered to do this for us. He could do it because he was without sin. He could also choose to overcome death brought on by the transgression of Adam in partaking of the forbidden fruit and thereby becoming mortal. Since Christ had power to choose to live or die, he could pay the price of this transgression.

Lucifer also volunteered to come to earth to provide the means for us to return to our Father in Heaven. But rather than paying for any sins we might commit here on earth, he would have forced us to obey each and every commandment, with no choice of our own. We would have no agency; we would be like robots that have no mind of their own. Returning to our Father in Heaven under this plan would then not be our free choice. Lucifer (who is also known as Satan) also wanted the glory that belonged to our Heavenly Father. His willful rebellion against our Father's plan (denying the agency of man), together with his desire for the Father's glory, resulted in the worst sin that has ever been committed by any of the children of God. Lucifer or Satan and was cast out of Heavenly Father's presence forever. His final state will be without a body, living forever in outer darkness, which means outside the presence of God and his influence eternally. Along with Satan, one third of Heavenly Father's children were cast out also, having willfully chosen to follow Satan and, like him, never to have a body of flesh and bones.

By Heavenly Father's wanting the "glory" does not mean he wants the credit. He wants us to return to him. His "work and *glory* is to bring to pass the immortality and eternal life of man" (Moses 1:39).

Jesus Christ and Michael created the world under the direction of the Father. Michael (also known as Adam) and Eve were this earth's first human spirits to receive bodies. Jesus later came to earth to pay for Adam's transgression as well as to pay the sins of all mankind. We have to repent and do our best to keep the commandments to be forgiven and escape the need to pay for our own sins.

Jesus organized his Church on earth and in the spirit world where all mankind go after the physical body dies. In order for everyone who ever lived on the earth to have the opportunity to accept the Gospel or the plan of salvation and to receive the holy ordinances required to return to our Father, the Savior has extended the blessings of the Atonement to those who would repent even after this life is over. For this to be effective, we who remain on earth, have the responsibility of performing vicariously the saving ordinances of the temple for these, our brothers and sisters.

In this life and after this life, in paradise and in spirit prison, all mankind will have the opportunity to continue to progress and accomplish the purposes of mortality. After the 1,000-year Millennium, we will pass through the Judgment where we will be assigned to one of God's kingdoms (Celestial, Terrestrial, or Telestial) according to that which we have become worthy. Those in the Celestial kingdom will continue to progress like our Heavenly Father, and become like him and be with their families eternally.

As a tenth and culminating blessing, ***everything that Heavenly Father has*** will be ours, if we fully repent of our sins and endure to the end. There is no reason to worry about our handfuls of dust in the form of houses, automobiles, fine clothing and other earthly, material things, when we can have everything the Lord has. As the scriptures promise the faithful: "All that my Father hath shall be given unto him" (D&C 84:38).

Years ago, there was a very wealthy man who, with his devoted young son, shared a passion for art collecting. Together they traveled around the world, adding only the finest treasures of art to their collection. Priceless works by Renoir, Monet, Van Gogh, Picasso, and many others adorned the walls of the family estate. The widowed, elderly man looked on with satisfaction as his only child became an experienced art collector. The son's trained eye and sharp business mind caused his father to beam with pride as they dealt with art collectors around the world.

War engulfed the nation and the young man left to serve his country. After a few short weeks, his father received a telegram that his beloved son was missing in action. The art collector anxiously awaited more news, fearing he would never see his son again. Within days, his fears were confirmed. The young man had died while rushing a fellow soldier to a medic. Distraught and lonely, the old man lived each day with anguish and sadness.

Some time later, a knock on the door awakened the depressed man. He was greeted by a soldier with a large package in his hands. He introduced himself to the man, saying he "was a friend of your son. I was the one he was rescuing when he died. May I come in for a few moments? I have something to show you."

As the two men spoke, the young soldier said, "I am an artist and I want to give you this." As the older man unwrapped the package, the paper gave way to reveal a portrait of the man's son. Though the world would never consider it the work of a genius, the painting featured the young man's face in striking detail. Overcome with emotion, the man thanked the soldier, promising to hang the portrait above the fireplace.

During the days and weeks that followed, the man realized that even though his son was no longer with him, the young man's life would live on because of those whom he had touched. He would soon learn that his son had rescued dozens of wounded soldiers before a bullet stilled his caring heart. The painting of the man's son soon became his most prized possession, eclipsing any interest in the pieces for which museums around the world clamored. He told his neighbors it was the greatest gift he had ever received.

The following spring, the old man became ill and passed away. The art world waited with great anticipation! The man's collection would be auctioned. The day soon arrived and art collectors from around the world gathered to bid on some of the world's most spectacular paintings. Dreams would be fulfilled this day. Greatness would be achieved as many would claim, "I now have the greatest collection."

The auction began with a painting that was not on any museum list. It was the portrait of the man's son. The auctioneer asked for an opening bid. "Who will open the bidding with $100?" he asked. The room was silent. Minutes passed. No one spoke. From the back of the room came a question: "Who cares about that painting? It's just a picture of his son. Forget it and go on to the masterpieces." Voices echoed in agreement.

"No. First we must sell this," replied the auctioneer. "Now, who will take the son?"

Finally, a friend of the old man spoke up. "Will you take ten dollars for the painting? That's all I have. I knew the boy, so I'd like to have it."

"I have ten dollars. Will anyone go higher?" called the auctioneer. After more silence, the auctioneer said, "Going once, going twice. Gone." The gavel fell.

Cheers filled the room and someone exclaimed, "Now we can get on with it and bid on these treasures!" The auctioneer looked at the audience and announced that the auction was over. Stunned disbelief quieted the room. Someone spoke up and asked, "What do you mean it's over? We didn't come here for a picture of some old man's son. What about these masterpieces? There are millions of dollars of art here! We demand that you explain what's going on here!"

The auctioneer replied, "It's very simple. According to the will of the father, whoever took the son would get it all."

This summarizes the Gospel of Jesus Christ. According to the will of the Father, whoever takes the Son, gets it all.[19]

A few of the great blessings of the Church and the Gospel are taking care of each other; we are like a family worldwide. We have the fruits of the Church, the joys of service, the blessings of obedience to the commandments, and ongoing revelation. The Church follows the blueprint described in the Bible and we have additional scriptures to guide and comfort us. We have the gifts of the priesthood and the Gift of the Holy Ghost. We have the plan of salvation and everything Heavenly Father has shall be ours. May we appreciate these great blessings and share them with others is my humble hope and prayer.

Notes:

1. Le Quotidien du Medicine, French periodical article in possession of the author. See also: *Encyclopedia of Mormonism*, MacMillan Publishing Co., New York, 1992; p. 1584.
2. Article in possession of the author. See also: *Encyclopedia of Mormonism*, MacMillan Publishing Co., New York, 1992 p. 1584, which states that the incidence is thirty to eighty percent lower than among non-Mormons.

3. *Statistical Abstract of the United States: 1999,* Government Printing Office, Washington D.C., 1999, Table 141.
4. *Ibid.* Table 132.
5. *Ibid.* Table 102.
6. *Ibid.* Table 95.
7. *Ibid.* Table 277.
8. *Ibid.* Table 267.
9. Petersen, Mark E., *Ensign,* The Church of Jesus Christ of Latter-day Saints, Salt Lake City, November 1975; pp. 63-65.
10. "LDS Rank High in Marriage, Low in Divorce," *Ensign,* The Church of Jesus Christ of Latter-day Saints, Salt Lake City, July 1984; pp. 78-80. See also: *Encyclopedia of Mormonism,* MacMillan Publishing Co., New York; 1992 pp. 392, 393. See also: Lobdell, Wiliam, "In Year of Divorce, Mormon Temple Weddings Are Built to Last," *Los Angeles Times,* Los Angeles, April 8, 2000.
11. "Our Brothers' Keepers," *Ensign,* The Church of Jesus Christ of Latter-day Saints, Salt Lake City, June 1998; p. 32.
12. Wirthlin, Joseph B., "Inspired Church Welfare," *Ensign,* The Church of Jesus Christ of Latter-day Saints, Salt Lake City, May 1999; pp. 76-78.
13. Benson, Ezra Taft, General Conference, April 1987, *Ensign,* The Church of Jesus Christ of Latter-day Saints, Salt Lake City, May 1987; p. 85.
14. Benson, Ezra Taft, General Conference, April 1986, *Ensign,* The Church of Jesus Christ of Latter-day Saints, Salt Lake City, May 1986; p. 78.
15. Benson, Ezra Taft, General Conference, April 1987, *Ensign,* The Church of Jesus Christ of Latter-day Saints, Salt Lake City, May 1987; p. 85.
16. Romney, Marion G., General Conference, April 1980 *Ensign,* The Church of Jesus Christ of Latter-day Saints, Salt Lake City, May 1980; p. 67.
17. *Family Home Evening Manual,* Council of Twelve Apostles of The Church of Jesus Christ of Latter-day Saints, Salt Lake City, 1965; p. iii.
18. Wirthlin, Joseph B., General Conference, April 1999, *Ensign,* The Church of Jesus Christ of Latter-day Saints, Salt Lake City, May 1999; p. 76.
19. Story of unknown authorship.

10
Logic

"Come now, and let us reason together, saith the Lord" (Isaiah 1:18). Elder Boyd K. Packer said: "Each of us must accommodate the mixture of reason and revelation in our lives. The gospel not only permits but requires it." [1]

After dating Kathie Taylor for a short time, I fell madly in love and I knew she was "the one" for me. It took her several months longer to come to the same conclusion. After trying to talk and reason with her many times without making much progress in convincing her that we should get married, I was at a loss for what to do.

I knew Kathie's favorite flower was the lilac. One day, I asked my younger sisters to help me fill my Volkswagen Beetle to the roof with lilacs in every place imaginable inside the car. Then I drove about thirty minutes to Kathie's home, peeking through the flowers, nearly passing out from the fragrance of lilacs. When I arrived I knocked on her door. She answered and I just pointed to the car. Her heart, as well as her mother's, was touched.

When the Lord wants to tell us something, he frequently speaks to our heart. This is generally the way we receive a testimony of the truthfulness of the Gospel. Sometimes, however, he speaks to our mind. He said:

And now come, saith the Lord and let us reason together, that ye may understand. Let us reason even as a man reasoneth one with another face to face. Now, when a man reasoneth he is understood of man, because he reasoneth as a man; even so will I, the Lord reason with you that you may understand (D&C 50:10-12).

Six times in three verses the Lord used the word reason. "Come now, and let us reason together, saith the Lord" (Isaiah 1:18). The Lord also said:

Behold, thou knowest that thou hast inquired of me and I did enlighten thy mind; and now I tell thee these things that thou mayest know that thou hast been enlightened by the Spirit of truth . . . if you desire a further witness, cast your mind upon the night that you cried unto me in your heart, that you might know concerning the truth of these things. Did I not speak peace to your mind concerning the matter? What greater witness can you have than from God? (D&C 6:15; 22, 23).

Here the Lord emphasized speaking to the mind, not just the heart. As those who investigate the Church consider baptism, they ask in prayer about whether the Church is true. They must remember that the Spirit often speaks to the mind as well as to the heart.

I have a simple mind. For me there are many things in the world that do not make sense. Even if the Spirit had not born witness to my heart about the truthfulness of the Gospel as taught in the Church, which it certainly has on hundreds of occasions, I would probably have joined the Church just because its doctrines are logical. They make sense to me. They answer the questions in my mind. Some of these doctrines are as follows:

I have attended many weddings in which the pastor has said to the couple, "Till death do you part," or "You are married as long as you both shall live." This is the doctrine all other churches preach with regard to marriage. To me it makes no sense that we should spend our whole life learning to love our spouse more and more deeply, to care for him or her even more than we care for ourselves, then have the relationship end at death. I cannot conceive of a true heaven where I cannot be with my beloved wife for eternity. Anything less than that would not be heaven to me. I do not believe that God intends to have us be single forever when so much joy and happiness comes through marriage and family relationships.

The death of a child or a parent or other family member presents another problem in logic, as far as I am concerned. We see so much tragedy on the earth such as when small children are killed. We feel great sorrow when one of our parents dies. It does not make any sense to me that we will never see them again. Does it make sense that a loving God would permit such tragedies then never allow us to see our children or parents again?

Almost every week, I hear about persons who have died and relatives or friends say these people are now with their parents who died previously. Or, they say those who have died are with their grandparents in heaven. Or, they might say they are with their child who went before them. Movies often portray this idea—that families will be together after this life. Newspaper and magazine stories frequently quote people who state that they know they will be with their loved ones in heaven. I think most people believe that this is true. This is part of the light of Christ, which is given to all who are born into the world. It is one of the beautiful truths that everyone innately knows, even though no other church teaches it.

I cannot imagine going to heaven and seemingly sitting on a cloud strumming a harp for all eternity. Does such a thing make any sense at all? That is, in essence, what other churches teach today. They teach that we will simply sing praises to God forevermore. Certainly, we will praise our Heavenly Father forever but that is not the only thing we will do. In my mind, I can only conceive a heaven where we continue to grow; where we learn and gain additional knowledge; where we progress to a higher level of spirituality; where we become like our Father and Mother in Heaven. It makes sense to me that God is my father; that I was created in his image (Genesis 1:27); that I am a joint heir with Christ (Romans 8:17); and that I have the opportunity to become like my Father. I will be able to progress eternally.

How can anyone believe that our lives *began* at our birth into this world and that there was no life before this one? Does that make any sense? All of us are so different from each other. We were born under different circumstances and at different times and places. Some were born five thousand years ago in the middle of Mongolia or in central Africa. Some are born today under privileged circumstances. Some are born with great handicaps. Some are born possessing certain outstanding talents or gifts. Some are born with yellow skin, others with black skin, others with red or brown or white skin. Some are born into great poverty and suffering while others are born into spectacular opulence. How can that be fair, given the fact that we have a loving Heavenly Father? If life began at birth into this world, all this does not make any sense to me.

The poet Wordsworth wrote:

> Our birth is but a sleep and a forgetting;
> The soul that rises with us, our life's star,
> Hath had elsewhere its setting,
> And cometh from afar;
> Not in entire forgetfulness,
> And not in utter nakedness,
> But trailing clouds of glory do we come
> From God who is our home.[2]

It makes sense that our progression as spirits in a pre-mortal exis-tence would, in some way, determine our circumstances on earth. If we did not live before coming to earth, how is our Heavenly Father actually our Father? The scriptures say we are literally his spirit chil-dren (Romans 8:16). That means we lived as spirits before we obtained a body.

Many Christian churches believe that only those who know and accept Jesus Christ in this life can be saved. If they also believe that God is loving and fair, this belief does not make sense. What about the billions of people who have never heard of Jesus Christ? There have been at least 95 billion of the 100 billion people who have lived on the earth that fall into that category through no fault of their own. Are they all automatically damned? That does not make any sense to me.

There has to be a way for everyone who has ever lived on earth to have a chance to accept or reject the Gospel of Jesus Christ. In the same way, there has to be a way that those who accept the Gospel in the next life have a chance to receive the earthly ordinances such as baptism that are required. It only makes sense. We are the only Church that preaches how this can be done—how those who have not had the chance on earth to be baptized and receive other impor-tant ordinances may receive the Gospel in the next life and have a valid baptism performed on their behalf.

Some Christian churches believe baptism is essential, others do not. Some believe the Bible is word-for-word perfect, others do not. It just stands to reason that not all of these churches can be right or that even two of them are both right. If a church preaches that bap-tism is essential in order to enter into heaven, its teaching is either correct or incorrect. It cannot be correct simply for those who believe in it yet not be correct for others.

Virtually all Protestant churches teach that there is more than one road to heaven and that there is not one true church. Yet all these churches disagree with each other as far as doctrines and teachings are concerned. It does not make sense that they could all be right or that even two different churches could be right. The Bible speaks of "One Lord, one faith, one baptism" (Ephesians 4:5). Surely it makes sense that Heavenly Father has established one right way and that there can only be one true church.

Heavenly Father has spoken to his children through prophets since the world was created. This is called revelation. God the

Father and Jesus Christ spoke to Adam and Eve. Jehovah spoke to Noah, Abraham, and Moses. He spoke to Elijah, Elisha, Isaiah, and Malachi. He also spoke to John the Baptist. When the Savior was on the earth, Heavenly Father spoke to him and Jesus spoke to his Father. After Jesus ascended into heaven, he continued to direct the Church and lead Heavenly Father's children through prophets. He spoke to Peter, to Paul, and to John. He and his Father appeared to Stephen. It does not make sense that this revelation would suddenly end, that Heavenly Father would not love us as much as he loved his children in ancient times. No other church today believes in prophets. Even the Catholic Church decreed in 1870 that the pope does not receive revelation; he only interprets ancient scripture.

We have as much need for a prophet as mankind ever did, perhaps more. This is one reason why there are literally thousands of churches today, each preaching its leader's own beliefs. It makes sense that Heavenly Father would call a prophet to lead us today, that God is the same yesterday, today and forever (1 Nephi 10:18). As Amos said in the Bible, "Surely the Lord God will do nothing but he revealeth his secret unto his servants the prophets" (Amos 3:7).

It does not make sense that there is just one heaven and one hell. Certainly there are many who deserve to go to a place called "heaven" and there are many who deserve to go to a place called "hell." But where does one draw the line between the two? Think about the difference between the last person to get into heaven and the next person who didn't quite make it? It does not make sense that there would be a hard line drawn; one person getting into heaven for all eternity and the next person who, perhaps, having prayed one fewer time or having gone to church one fewer Sunday or, perhaps, having told one more fib, would be consigned to hell for all eternity. That does not make any sense.

It does not make any sense that a person who is fortunate to receive his last rites before dying will go to heaven or be condemned to fewer years in purgatory than the person who died five minutes before his priest arrived. To me it makes sense that there are many levels in heaven, that we will each be where we can be the happiest. Surely this makes more sense when we believe that our Father in Heaven is a loving, compassionate, caring, merciful God.

It does not make sense to me that some Protestant churches teach that we are predestined, that nothing we do on earth can make any difference, that we were each assigned to heaven or hell even before we are born. These churches preach that we are saved solely by the grace of Christ, as though it is solely according to his good pleasure. Such a belief logically argues that there are certain ones of God's children that the Savior likes and others that he doesn't like. There's not good reason for that, that is just the way it is. This does not makes sense.

It makes sense that we need to do the best we can, that we need to obey the commandments of Jesus Christ. It makes sense to me that it is by grace as well as by our faith and our works that we are saved. As James said, "Faith without works is dead" (James 2:20). Faith, works, and the grace of Christ are all required to return to our Heavenly Father. And the Savior's grace applies to all who have faith in his word and follow him. In other words, those who truly love him and obey him demonstrate by their behavior that they want to be with him in the world to come. Those who do not have faith and obey his word show by their actions that they want to be in a place other than where he is.

It does not make sense that just anyone who wants to can direct Christ's church here on earth. When Jesus Christ called his apostles he said, "Ye have not chosen me, but I have chosen you" (John 15:16). Then he laid his hands on their heads and ordained them (see Mark 3:14, 15; John 15:16). One must be called as was Aaron; that is, he must be called by a prophet and ordained by the laying on of hands (Hebrews 5:4). Yet today, anyone who chooses can go to divinity school and become a minister, pastor, priest, or preacher. (Actually, there is nothing to keep a person from just declaring himself to be a clergyman and organizing a church). The ordination by the laying on of hands by one with authority simply is not necessary in other churches.

Most churches today teach that there is one God yet three Gods, that there are three Gods yet one God. This does not make any sense. When Christ was on the earth did he continually pray to himself? In the Garden of Gethsemane when he said, "Not my will but thine" (Luke 22:42), was he speaking to himself? When he was on the cross and said, "Father, into thy hands I commend my spirit" (Luke 23:46), was he talking to himself? There must be three separate and distinct Gods with a single, unified purpose: That purpose is to help us return to our Father in Heaven.

We have a Heavenly Father and were created in his image. It makes sense that we have a Heavenly Mother, too. It makes sense that he created us also in the image of our Heavenly Mother, that we are literally the spirit children of our Heavenly Parents. Other churches teach that this is blasphemy, that it somehow diminishes God. Heavenly Father is omniscient and represents everything that is good. It makes sense to me that he has a wife.

After Christ was resurrected he showed his body of flesh and bones to hundreds of his followers. Did he then give up his body once more? Virtually all churches today preach that God is only a spirit, that he has no body. Then what was the purpose of the crucifixion and resurrection? Why did he rise from the grave *with* his body? How were our bodies created in God's image if he does not have a body but is only a spirit? We know that Christ will return again with his body (Acts 1:11). It only makes sense that Christ has his body today just as we will have our bodies when we are resurrected.

When Christ was on the earth, he organized a specific church with apostles and prophets as its cornerstone. He also called others to serve in different positions or offices such as bishops, seventies, elders and priests. The Church had the Melchizedek Priesthood and the Aaronic Priesthood. No other church has this same organization today. Why not? Should we not be organized the way Christ's Church was organized?

In 325 A.D. at the Council of Nicea, several hundred representatives voted on whether God had a body or not. They voted on whether there were three Gods or just one God. They also officially formed the Catholic Church. Protestant churches were formed when certain leaders in the church protested against certain teachings or doctrines and broke off from the Catholic Church. In essence, the leaders of each of these churches decided or voted on various doctrines. Even today, if you do not like what one minister teaches, you can go across the street and find a church with which you agree. Is not this, in essence, voting on which doctrines are true? The ministers, pastors and, in some cases, bishops in most churches are chosen by their congregations. The people choose those pastors who have the same beliefs as they do. This does not make sense. Either a teaching or doctrine is true or it is not. How can man vote to determine which doctrines are true for Christ's church?

The Bible was compiled in the fourth century A.D. as a collection of writings of some of the ancient prophets who lived in

Palestine. The Dead Sea Scrolls and other ancient records clearly show there are many errors in the present-day Bibles and that there were many other writings of ancient prophets that were not included in the Bible. Are these other writings not important? Does it not make sense that God would call prophets to lead his children who live in other parts of the world and that they would also write the word of God as it has been given to them? It makes sense that there should be more than one set of scriptures that are a witness of the divinity of Jesus Christ. As the Bible says, "In the mouth of two or three witnesses shall every word be established" (2 Corinthians 13:1).

If a church is built around its organizer and leader, should it not be named after that leader? It does not make sense that some Christian churches are named after a street, or after a doctrine, or after an area of the city, or after one particular principle. It does make sense that the Church of Jesus Christ should be called by his name, i.e., "The Church of Jesus Christ." In the New Testament, "saints" were disciples of Christ and members of the Church of Jesus Christ. To distinguish us from the "former-day saints," we are called "The Church of Jesus Christ of Latter-day Saints." It only makes sense.

When the pope of the Catholic Church dies the various cardinals from around the world meet together to elect a new pope by majority vote. This frequently requires several ballots. If a Protestant minister or pastor should die or leave his church, the members of the parish vote on a new one. It makes sense that the Church of Jesus Christ should have leaders selected from the "top" not from the "bottom." They should be selected by Jesus Christ himself through his representatives. If a bishop or leader dies, his replacement should be indicated by revelation and inspiration from God.

Jesus Christ said many times that the Gospel should be preached to every nation, kindred, tongue and people (Mark 16:15, 16). The Gospel is not meant for only a few of Heavenly Father's children. The true church should be a missionary church making every effort to spread the blessings of the Gospel to all mankind.

In the New Testament the apostles and leaders of the Church were unpaid. It makes sense that we should not have a professional, paid clergy. The officers of the Church in the New Testament were married (See 1 Timothy 3:2; 4:3). It makes sense that in order to be able to counsel members with understanding, bishops, pastors and other leaders should not be prohibited from marrying and having a family.

There is only one place on earth where all of these questions are answered adequately. I testify that The Church of Jesus Christ of Latter-day Saints provides those answers. The Spirit does not always have to speak in a revelatory, witnessing sort of way. It often speaks in a simple, logical voice about what is right and what makes sense and I invite you to study and pray about these things if you are seeking to know the truth.

Notes:

1. Packer, Boyd K., "'I Say unto You, Be One'" (D&C 38:27), *Devotionals and Fireside Speeches,* Brigham Young University, Provo, Utah, 1991; p. 89.
2. Wordsworth, William, "Ode: Intimations of Immortality from Recollections of Early Childhood," *The Complete Poetical Works of William Wordsworth,* Macmillan, London, 1924; p. 359.

11
The Spirit

The witness of the Spirit is the ultimate evidence of the true Church.

In 1921, Elders David O. McKay and Hugh Cannon were touring the missions of the Church in the world. They were in Hawaii and decided they would visit the Kilauea Volcano one evening with about ten other brethren. One of the elders discovered a volcanic balcony about four feet down inside the crater where observers could look at the molten lava without being chilled by the cold wind at that high elevation. After being in this protected spot for some time, suddenly Brother McKay said, "Brethren, I feel impressed that we should get out of here." Assisting each other, they got out. Then, almost immediately, the whole balcony crumbled and fell with a roar into the molten lava a hundred feet below.[1]

After the mobs succeeded in driving the Saints out of Missouri, Joseph Smith went to the President of the United States, Martin Van Buren, and asked for assistance from the harm they had suffered. The President asked Joseph what the difference was between The Church of Jesus Christ of Latter-day Saints and all other churches. Joseph simply said that we have the Gift of the Holy Ghost.[2]

There are many other things Joseph could have said in terms of the differences between our Church and others. For example, he could have said that we have a prophet at the head of the Church; that we have twelve apostles like the twelve that Jesus chose; that we believe in eternal marriage and in sealing families together for eternity; and that we believe in three kingdoms of glory after this life as was taught by Paul.

The Prophet could have told the President that we believe in a paradise and a spirit prison after this life where those who did not hear the Gospel of Jesus Christ in this world will have the opportunity to be taught these truths after they die; that we perform baptisms, marriages and family sealings by proxy for those who have died and who accept the Gospel in the next world; and that we search out our ancestors, all the way back to Adam, so we can perform these ordinances for them.

He could have told the President that we have holy temples such as were known in the Bible, which are different from meetinghouses; that in such temples we perform sacred ordinances for ourselves and for our ancestors; that we believe in ongoing revelation; that we have a complete organization like the Church of Jesus Christ had as reported in the Bible, with elders, seventies, bishops, patriarchs and other offices; and that we have priesthood authority with a direct line back to Jesus Christ himself.

Joseph could have told President Van Buren that we believe in both the Melchizedek Priesthood and the Aaronic Priesthood as taught in the scriptures; that we believe in a pre-mortal life where we all lived with Heavenly Father and Jesus Christ before this life; that we believe we can continue to progress eternally and even become gods and have eternal increase; and that we believe in healing those who are ill using consecrated olive oil, as mentioned in the Bible.

He could have told the President that we believe in miracles; that we believe in the resurrection for everyone who has ever lived on the earth; that we have a health code known as the Word of Wisdom; that we pay tithing as taught in the scriptures; and that we believe we are saved by both works and grace.

He could have said that we believe in three separate beings in the Godhead; that we believe Heavenly Father and Jesus Christ have bodies of flesh and bones and that we were created in their image, and the Holy Ghost is a third member of the Godhead; and that we follow the other commandments in the scriptures, such as keeping the Sabbath holy and strict sexual fidelity.

Joseph could have said that we have scriptures in addition to the Bible; that we have the "Stick of Joseph" as spoken of by Ezekiel; that we believe that after Christ's resurrection 2,000 years ago, he appeared to the people in the western hemisphere to teach his "other sheep"; and that we believe that children are pure when they are born and they should not be baptized until the age of accountability, which is when they are eight years old.

He could have told the President we believe in baptism by immersion; that the Church bears the name of Jesus Christ; that the Church was restored in the form that the Savior organized it when he was on the earth, and that it did not break off from another church.

It would have been possible for him to say that we have no paid clergy; and that members of the Church all participate and have assignments or "callings."

Joseph could have told President Van Buren that we have missionaries around the world who, at their own expense, teach the Gospel to all people; that we fast or go without food and drink for two meals once a month and then contribute funds to help the poor; that we have a complete and independent welfare program to help those in need; and that we have the complete plan of our Heavenly Father and we know where we came from, why we are here on earth and where we are going.

Rather than mentioning any of the above, Joseph simply said that we have the Gift of the Holy Ghost. Although the light of Christ is given to all men to teach us right from wrong (Luke 15:8), the Gift of the Holy Ghost is something different. A person who is not a member of the Church may be touched by the Holy Ghost from time to time to testify to him of the truth, but the Gift of the Holy Ghost is bestowed on an individual only by the laying on of hands following baptism by one who has the authority (Acts 8:17). Then, through worthiness, we are entitled to its constant companionship.

The laying on of hands for the Gift of the Holy Ghost was an integral part of the Church Christ organized when he was on the earth. The Holy Ghost comforts us and gives us strength. He teaches and protects us. He witnesses to us of truth and guides us. He is with us on a constant basis if we remain worthy.

Over the past many years, I have written the ten preceding chapters of this book relating to evidences of the true Church. These chapters are like ten pieces of a cake that fit together as evidences of the truth. However, the best part of the cake is the frosting, which overshadows all the pieces and is smooth, rich, and creamy. The frosting on my cake is the Gift of the Holy Ghost. If you have tasted of this Spirit, you do not need to know the ingredients of the cake. You do not need to know anything else. Living by this Spirit alone will get you back to your Heavenly Father. Following are some of the roles of the Holy Ghost:

The Holy Ghost protects us. After spending two and a half years in New England and Canada helping the Saints move west, Wilford Woodruff traveled from Boston with 100 of the last members to leave. They arrived in Pittsburgh at dusk and were anxious to go on to St. Louis. Elder Woodruff spoke with the captain of a steamer who said they could take the whole group that night. However, the Spirit told him to not go aboard that steamer but to wait until the next morning. Within thirty minutes of the departing of the steamer, it burst into flame. Everyone aboard was killed. If Elder Woodruff had not obeyed the influence of the still small voice, all of the Saints with whom he was traveling would have been killed.[3]

When our children were small Kathie and I sometimes took them out on North Moline Street in Aurora, Colorado to watch airplanes take flight and others land directly over their heads. One day, she took the children there and got out of the car to watch the planes. The Spirit told her that she should leave immediately, which she did not want to do since they had just arrived. But instead, she listened, put the children back in the car, and left. Five minutes later, a plane crashed into this area.

I was driving to work one day when I felt a spirit come over me that told me something bad was about to happen. I immediately slowed down, then prayed aloud. I said, "Father, I do not know what is going to happen but I ask Thee to protect me." A car in the next lane suddenly swerved into my lane missing me by just an inch or so. Then I felt the sweet spirit of the Holy Ghost assuring me that I had been protected.

Frequently, the Lord uses other people to answer our prayers as well as to protect us. Let me give you an example of this. My father was not active in the Church for more than twenty years. The bishop of our ward came to our home and asked if my dad would visit a young couple once a month who had just moved in. He asked Dad if he would just see if he could help in any way. My father agreed to do so.

He was a bit resentful, but Dad went to the small trailer house. He could hear a baby crying as he knocked on the door. A young woman answered it. She was carrying the baby and it was obvious that she was expecting a second child. It was also obvious that she had been crying. She invited my father into the very small living room, which was filled with undone washing and ironing, diapers, towels, and sheets. He found a small box to sit on as the young mother began to cry.

"I got married far too young. My baby is always sick. I'm sixteen years old and I'm seven months pregnant with my second child. I'm always sick. My husband works three jobs and I never see him. We have not been to Church. Life is just terrible!"

After a short time my father left the home, thinking that he had made the girl feel uncomfortable and that he had been an imposition. He told himself he would not return. My mother told Dad to call the bishop, which he did. The bishop asked him to return to visit the young woman the following month and report back to him. The same thing happened again. There was a sick baby, a mother who had been crying, and laundry that needed work. The girl cried and cried. My father left vowing again not to return.

The following Sunday was Fast Sunday. My father had not attended Church meetings in over twenty years except for just a few minutes when one of his children was to be confirmed or given a name and a blessing. On these occasions, he would sit on the back row and leave immediately after the ordinance was performed. That particular Sunday, my baby sister, Marcy, was to be blessed. The bishop asked Dad if he would stand in the circle in the front, which he did. Immediately after the blessing, he realized he could not walk out in front of everyone, so he sat down in the front row.

In the middle of the testimony meeting, he heard a familiar voice from the back of the chapel. A young woman began her words with: "I got married far too young. My baby is always sick. I have been continually sick and will deliver another child in the next few days. My husband works three jobs and I rarely see him." She then said, "There have been two times in my life when I felt I might do something drastic to myself and my children. Each time, I prayed as hard as I could and each time the Lord answered my prayer by sending someone to help me. He sent Brother Brown." As a result of this experience, my father became active in the Church.

The Holy Ghost teaches us with messages from our heavenly home to show us the way. Following are a few of the principles the Holy Ghost has taught me. When Adam was driven out of the Garden of Eden, he built an altar to offer sacrifices. After many days, an angel asked him why he did this and he said, "I know not save the Lord commanded me" (Moses 5:6).

How many days does it take to qualify for "after many days ?" It might have been 100 days or 100 years. We do not know. We do know, however, that without knowing the reasons why, Adam was faithful and obedient throughout that whole time. As a result of his obedience the entire Gospel was revealed to him. Precise obedience brings great blessings. We obey, not out of "blind faith," but because our eyes are open to the truth of the Gospel.

My experience in keeping the commandments has led me to believe in what I call an "eighty-twenty law of the Gospel." I would say that when people keep 80% of a commandment, they receive just 20% of the blessings. When they keep the last 20%, they receive the other 80% of the blessings.

As an example, let's say that you decide to keep all of the Word of Wisdom except for drinking one glass of wine each week. By giving up tobacco, coffee, tea, and most alcohol, you will receive some blessings. However, the **rich** blessings of obedience come when you finally give up that last glass of wine. If you keep only 80% of the Word of Wisdom, you will get only 20% of the blessings. If you pay 80% of your tithing, you will get just 20% of the blessings. Rich blessings result from precise obedience.

We must ask for the blessings we desire and need. The scriptures do not say, "It will be given you; ye shall find; it will be opened unto you." Rather, they say, "*Ask*, and it will be given you; *seek*, and ye shall find; *knock*, and it will be opened unto you." In other words, you have to do your part—the Lord doesn't just give you what you want; you have to ask and to work, too.

In The Book of Mormon, Moroni wrote a beautiful promise.

Behold, I would exhort you that when ye shall read these things that you ask God, the Eternal Father, in the name of Christ, if these things are not true; and if ye shall ask with a sincere heart, with real intent, having faith in Christ, he will manifest the truth of it unto you by the power of the Holy Ghost (Moroni 10:3, 4).

What are the keys to Moroni's promise that you can know The Book of Mormon is true? First you must *read* it. Next, you have to *ask* Heavenly Father if it is true. But you must ask with a *sincere heart* and with *real intent*. It also requires *faith in Jesus Christ*. After you have read the book, the next four steps you take relate to asking and *how* you ask.

The sacred ordinances are absolutely required for entering the kingdom of God after this life. There are millions of wonderful people in the world who are not members of The Church of Jesus Christ of Latter-day Saints. However, no matter how good a person is, he must be baptized by proper authority in order to enter into the kingdom of heaven. No matter how righteous a person is, he must receive the ordinances of the temple by the proper authority.

We each have ministering angels who watch over us. Approximately 100 billion people have lived on the earth. Since one third of the hosts of heaven were cast out, this means there are at least 50 billion evil spirits who followed Lucifer. There are now about six billion people on the earth, so there are at least eight evil spirits for every one of us. Certainly, many of these may be assigned by Satan to work in the spirit prison but, on the other hand, Satan probably believes that many people are "doing just fine" by themselves without the "help" of evil spirits to guide them. I can certainly feel those evil spirits who have been assigned to me. But I can feel even stronger the ministering angels who watch over me. Each angel has more power through the Holy Ghost than all of the evil spirits.

It is generally easiest to feel the Holy Ghost in calm, peaceful places since he often speaks to us in a still small voice. It is easy to drown out that voice by television or by loud music or by shouting. Although the world is getting more and more noisy and complex, we can hear the Holy Ghost more easily where it is quiet, peaceful and simple.

Elder Henry B. Eyring said: "Sin in any form offends the Holy Ghost. You must not do anything or go anywhere that offends the Spirit. You cannot afford that risk."[4] If we go to movies where we shouldn't be or listen to music we shouldn't listen to, or look at magazines or things on the Internet we should not look at, it is difficult to hear and feel the promptings of the Holy Ghost. If we feel or express contention toward another, it is difficult to feel the Spirit.

Sundays can often be difficult because we do not always keep the Spirit with us. When you feel the Spirit strongly in a Church meeting, you can be certain that within a few minutes or hours, Satan and his followers will try hard to counteract this feeling. That is their life's work. They will always want to counteract the influence of the Spirit. If you attend a wonderful, spiritual fast and testimony meeting, be assured that on the way home Satan and his angels will try to get your children to begin fighting and yelling in the car. He will also try to get dad and mom to become upset and yell back at the kids in an attempt to control them and their misbehavior. This contention drives away the Spirit.

Blessings often seem to come when times are most difficult. When our backs are to the wall and we are humbled, the windows of heaven begin to open and frequently we have the greatest spiritual experiences of our lives. If you pay your tithing when you know you will not have enough to eat for the rest of the month, something will happen to help you if you remain humble and seek the Spirit of the Lord. When you are truly down but sincerely seeking the Lord and his help (like the young woman whom my father visited), when you are the most humble spiritually, when you are in greatest need, the Spirit will come to carry you for awhile if your attitude is positive and you don't have a rebellious attitude. Remember, even when we're down and out, the Lord expects us to have a grateful heart.

We must forgive all men. The Holy Ghost simply cannot come into our lives and direct us if we insist on acting on unkind feelings toward anyone. Being human, there are times that others will do things that appear to us to be unkind, uncaring, unloving, hurtful, and even cruel. Sometimes it may appear that the things that offend us are done on purpose—and maybe they are. It is natural to have unkind and even mean thoughts come into our mind at such times. It is what we *do* with those thoughts that matters. The Lord commanded that we forgive all men their trespasses against us. We are not justified on getting even or taking vengeance. The best thing to do in such cases is to remember that Heavenly Father will bless our efforts to forgive those who spitefully use us and hurt us.

If you were bitten by a rattlesnake, you would not chase it down to seek vengeance. This will only accelerate the movement of the poison in your system. You must focus on calmly removing the poison as rapidly as possible. If someone has offended you and you feel like retaliating, you will only accelerate the movement of poison if you act on those impulses. Instead, concentrate on removing the poison by forgiving that person no matter what his motivation. The Lord will bless you in so doing and peace will come into your soul.

Service is magic. In service, we forget our personal problems, we overcome depression, we increase our self-esteem. It brings great blessings as God loves all his children and he may need you to help those in need. Satan would have us withhold our means and our substance. He would have us believe that such things are our own. But as King Benjamin said to his people, we are not justified in withholding our means from the beggar, even if we believe the beggar has brought his grief upon himself (Mosiah 4).

The Holy Ghost is our Comforter. Today, missionaries are not released from missionary service until they actually return home and receive their release from their stake presidents. I served a mission in France and Belgium in the mid-1960s. At that time, the mission president gave missionaries their release. Missionaries in those days often were allowed to travel after their mission president released them and prior to their returning home.

Following my mission, I purchased a Volkswagen Beetle and toured Europe with another released missionary. We obtained visas to visit Czechoslovakia and then wanted to go through East Germany to Berlin. At that time, Czechoslovakia and East Germany were behind the "Iron Curtain."

We drove from Vienna to the Czech border where we saw an electrified fence about ten-feet high with barbed wire on top. Men with automatic weapons approached us and checked our visas. They waved us through the gate. About 200 yards farther ahead, we came to another fence, about twelve-feet high. We were asked to get out of the car. The car was searched and we were required to purchase Czech insurance in order to continue on. We were given other papers, most of which we could not understand.

About 200 yards farther up the road, we came to a third fence, about fourteen-feet high. Several soldiers with machine guns quizzed us once more and finally waved us through. Driving to Prague on a narrow, cobblestone road, we saw only one gasoline pump in about 100 miles. The gasoline made my VW engine knock. As we drove into Prague that afternoon, it was very depressing. The only hotel room available was one with four beds; the other two beds were already taken by an East German and a Dutchman.

We went to the U.S. Embassy to obtain visas to enter East Germany. We were advised to leave Czechoslovakia by way of West Germany as rapidly as we could because several Americans had recently disappeared in Czechoslovakia and had not been found. As we were sitting in our car in front of the hotel talking about depressive Communism, a man approached us who spoke some French. He said he saw our Belgian license plates and wanted to exchange some money with us. We turned him down, but he said he collected foreign money and even if we had only a few foreign coins in our pockets, he would give us a good price. We did not see any harm in this, so we sold him a few German, Austrian, French and Swiss coins. He gave us double or triple the exchange rate in Czech crowns, then he ran down the street.

As we entered our hotel room talking about this strange occurrence, the Dutchman's eyes widened and he suggested we read the papers we had received upon entering the country. They said: *"It is strictly forbidden to exchange any money, except in a government bank, under penalty of imprisonment."* The Dutchman told us that Czech money was worthless outside the country. Czech people would try to exchange money on the street and sell it on the "black market" to anyone who might want to escape the country.

I was greatly disturbed. I tried to go to sleep. When I dozed off, I had a terrible nightmare about trying to leave the country. In my dream the guards at the border searched my car and then took us inside. They asked whether we had exchanged any money on the street. It was a great dilemma for me in my dream since I had just been released from my mission and knew that I had to tell the truth. Before I could answer, someone behind me laughed; it was the man on the street in a Communist uniform who was holding our coins.

I woke up in a cold sweat. After repeating the nightmare two or three times, I arose and read my patriarchal blessing that said I would marry in the Temple and be happy in my home with my wife and children. A great Spirit of comfort came over me and I realized this was the Holy Ghost telling me that everything would be okay.

We left very early for the West German border, very apprehensive of what might come next. We reached the gates, our passports were checked and we were simply waved through. We then cheered as we saw three different brands of gasoline stations.

In these troubled times of drugs, alcohol, materialism, poverty, abortion, crime, wars, strife, depression and stress, we have the Gift of the Holy Ghost to provide us great comfort by telling us that everything will be okay.

The Holy Ghost is a witness of the truth. One Thursday in 1999, shortly before I was released as mission president of the France Paris Mission, I received a phone call from a woman named Maryse. She said she needed to see me immediately so I asked her to come to the mission office. She told me the missionaries had taught her for eight years and had scheduled her for baptism on Saturday—two days away. She said she could not be baptized and she had come to me to explain her reasons so I would help the missionaries understand.

As we spoke, she said that she did not believe in the Church. She could not accept commandments such as tithing, the Word of Wisdom, the law of chastity, or the other requirements to become a member of the Church. She said she did not have a witness of the truth. We discussed the commandments one by one and she said that if she had a testimony, she would be willing to live according to these laws, however, she said she simply had had no feeling that the Church was true.

I said, "Maryse, you are sitting on holy ground. You are in the office of the president of one of the Savior's missions. This mission is directed by the Lord's angels. They are here in this office today. Let us kneel down together. You ask Heavenly Father if these things are true and if this is his Son's Church. Two minutes from now, you will feel something that you have never felt before. Then you will ask me for permission to be baptized on Saturday."

We knelt down together and she commenced to pray. After a minute or two, she began to cry. She cried and cried. Then she looked up at me and said, "This is marvelous! It is true, isn't it?! May I please be baptized on Saturday?"

Most people do not have a great revelatory experience like this. As Elder Dallin Oaks said, "With most people—especially those raised in the Church—gaining a testimony is not an event but a process."[5] Elder Bruce R. McConkie said, "Being born again is a gradual thing. As far as the generality of the members of the Church are concerned, we are born again by degrees, and we are born again to added light and added knowledge and added desires for righteousness as we keep the commandments."[6]

The Spirit speaks to us in many different voices. Here are examples of some of the voices. "Did I not speak *peace to your mind* concerning the matter? What greater witness can you have than from God?" (D&C 6:23). "I will tell you *in your mind and in your heart,* by the Holy Ghost . . . this is the spirit of revelation" (D&C 8:2, 3). "You must study it out in your mind; then you must ask me if it be right, and if it is right I will cause that your *bosom shall burn* within you" (D&C 9:8).

"Put your trust in that Spirit which *leadeth to do good*" (D&C 11:12). "My Spirit, . . . *shall enlighten your mind,* which shall *fill your soul with joy.*" (D&C 11:13). "The Holy Ghost, . . . which [is the] *Comforter . . . filleth with hope and perfect love*" (Moroni 8:26).

"Be led by the Holy Spirit, becoming *humble, meek, submissive, patient, full of love and all long-suffering*" (Alma 13:28). "[The] Holy Ghost, even the Comforter, . . . showeth all things, and *teacheth the peaceable things* of the kingdom" (D&C 39:6). "He hath spoken unto you in a *still small voice.* . . . ye could not *feel* his words." (1 Nephi 17:45).

"Thus saith the *still small* voice, which whispereth through and pierceth all things." (D&C 85:6)."[It was] not a harsh voice, neither was it a loud voice . . . notwithstanding it being a small voice . . . it did pierce them to the very soul, and did *cause their hearts to burn*" (3 Nephi 11:3). "But the fruit of the Spirit is *love, joy, peace, long-suffering, gentleness, goodness, faith, meekness, temperance*" (Galatians 5:22, 23).

The Holy Ghost provides spiritual gifts, as well as guidance and power. A number of years ago, through the power of the priesthood and the guidance of the Holy Ghost, Matthew Cowley, an apostle, raised a person from the dead. In another instance, he gave a blind person his eyesight.[7] I gave a priesthood blessing to a six-year-old who had a brain tumor the size of a softball or grapefruit. The doctor said she would live only a few months. Today she is thirty years old and well.

I gave a blessing to a man going into surgery. He had had a terrible accident and the doctor said that he would probably die but, if he lived, he would certainly have severe brain damage. The blessing said he would completely recover. He was released from the hospital within a few days and is normal today.

On at least ten occasions, I have given blessings to individuals who had abnormal lumps or growths or polyps. The Lord told each of them through me that they had been healed and that the lumps or growths or polyps had disappeared. In surgery the next few days, in each occasion, the doctors found nothing, although on the prior X-rays the growths were obvious.

I gave a blessing to a man in the hospital whom the doctors said would die from cancer within a few hours. He was released from the hospital the next day and lived for several months—long enough to get his temporal affairs for his family in order.

When I was a bishop, I sat in a Sacrament Meeting and silently selected out of a congregation a woman whom I thought would be an excellent Young Women's President. However, I was concerned about her husband's support. After the meeting this brother came up to me and said, "Bishop, the Spirit told me that you want my wife as Young Women's President. It is okay with me."

In 1998, I was in France when I taught the missionary discussions with the missionaries to a man named Riaz. They asked him to be baptized and he refused. He said he had studied the Church for nine years and knew that it was true but he was simply too comfortable to be burdened with commandments. Through the Spirit, I told him that within six months he would *lose* all these comforts. The next week, he failed every single one of his college exams, although previously he had been an excellent student. His family asked him to leave home and he lost almost everything. After a short time, he became humble and was baptized into the Church.

Another time when I was a bishop, I was trying to select a counselor. The only individual I focused on was Mike Dudley but I thought he was probably too young. After that, whenever I thought about who should fill the calling, my thoughts returned to Mike, but then thought that he was too young. One day while I was thinking about him, the phone rang. The person at the other end said, "Bishop, I just called to tell you that Mike Dudley is much more mature than his age might indicate and he could handle any calling in the Church that you might give him. Goodbye." Mike became a great counselor to me.

There is spiritual power in this work. Ordinary members of the Church, like us, having received the Gift of the Holy Ghost can actually do the work of the Lord. Brigham Young said: We should live so as to possess that Spirit daily, hourly, and every moment. That is a blessing to us, which makes the path of life easy."[8]

In a very spiritual meeting, when someone would comment to President Harold B. Lee that the veil was particularly thin that day, he would respond: "What veil?" or "There is no veil."[9] I testify to you through the Gift of the Holy Ghost that the Savior guides this Church today and that we can also be guided to conform our will to that of our Heavenly Father. We will then return to him as we follow the promptings of this great gift that we have been given.

Notes:

1. Middlemiss, Clare, Compiler, *Cherished Experiences from the Writings of President David O. McKay*, Deseret Book, Salt Lake City, 1970; p. 60.
2. Ludlow, Daniel H., BYU *Speeches of the Year 1963*, Brigham Young University, Provo, Utah, Nov. 12, 1963. See also: *History of the Church*, The Deseret Book Company, Salt Lake City, 1980; 4:42.
3. Stuy, Brian H., Ed., *Collected Discourses 1886-1898*, B.H.S. Publishing, Burbank, CA, 1987. See also: Arrington, Leonard J. Ed., *The Presidents of the Church*, Deseret Book, SLC, 1986; p. 129.
4. Eyring, Elder Henry B., General Conference, April 2001, *Ensign*, The Church of Jesus Christ of Latter-day Saints, Salt Lake City, May 2001.
5. Oaks, Dallin H., "Teaching and Learning by the Spirit," *Ensign*, The Church of Jesus Christ of Latter-day Saints, Salt Lake City, March 1997; p. 14.
6. McConkie, Bruce R., "Jesus Christ and Him Crucified," *Devotional Speeches of the Year*, Brigham Young University, Provo, Utah, 1976; p. 399.
7. Cowley, Matthew, *Matthew Cowley Speaks*, Deseret Book Company, Salt Lake City, 1954; pp. 237-249.
8. Young, Brigham, *Journal of Discourses*, Latter-day Saints Book Depot, London, England, 1886; 7:238.
9. Walsh, Jack, "D. Arthur Haycock: Aide to Four Prophets." *Ensign*, The Church of Jesus Christ of Latter-day Saints, Salt Lake City, August 1984; p. 23.

INDEX

About the Author

 Over the past 25 years, Dennis has served as the president of the France Paris Mission (1996-1999), eight years as counselor to three presidents of the Colorado Denver Mission and the Colorado Denver South Mission, ten years in stake presidencies of three stakes, and four years as a bishop. As a young man, he served in the Franco Belgian Mission.

He has always secretly desired to teach the Gospel Doctrine class in Sunday School. He received that calling after returning from France, but he served only one week before being called to serve in the bishopric of a young single adult ward, which calling he also loves.

Dennis has a B. S. degree in Computer Science and a B. A. degree in Mathematics from the University of Utah. He received a Masters of Business Administration (MBA) degree from Northwestern University.

During his twenty-three years in management consulting, Dennis has been retained as an Expert Witness in more than 150 civil litigation cases. His principal duties in this regard have been to evaluate, analyze and summarize evidence, and then testify.

He doesn't claim to be a scholar in terms of speaking ancient languages and performing original research. He has, however, read many hundreds of books and articles, and he enjoys succinctly summarizing the research of others and simplifying ideas for all to understand. He has given hundreds of Church talks and firesides, many about evidences of the true Church.

Dennis, and his wife, the former Kathleen Taylor, have lived in the Denver Colorado area for the past 30 years other than the three years presiding over the France Paris Mission. They have five children and ten grandchildren (so far).